STOP BURNOUT NOW

The Serenity Maven's Guide to Balanced Wellness

STOP BURNOUT NOW

STEPS, TIPS, & ACTIVITIES
How to Create Happiness and Balance
When You Are Sick and Tired From
Being Overwhelmed and Unfulfilled

HONEY-MARIE LOVE, RMT, MLC

Copyright © 2019 Honey-Marie Love, RMT, MLC.

This book is sold subject to the condition that it shall not, by way of trade or otherwise, be lent, re-sold, duplicated, hired out, or otherwise circulated without the publisher's and author's prior written consent in any form of binding or cover other than that in which it is published and without similar condition including this condition being imposed on the subsequent purchaser.

Stop Burnout Now - The Serenity Maven's Guide to Balanced Wellness
How to Create Happiness and Balance When You Are Sick and
Tired From Being Overwhelmed and Unfulfilled

All Rights Reserved
Copyright © November 2019 by Honey-Marie Love

Author:

A book by Honey-Marie Love, RMT, MLC

Published by Rising Above Publishing Services
Editor: Shareen Rivera
www.shareenrivera.com
Professional Author Photos© 2017 Erica Nichole Photography - Taken July 2017

ISBN-13: 9781702106153

Any characters and events portrayed are included at the creative license of the author's and any resemblance to actual events, or locales or persons, living or dead are entirely coincidental. The contents of this book are not intended to treat, cure, or prevent any medical condition, illness or disease.

All rights reserved. No part of this book may be reproduced, stored, or transmitted by any means—whether auditory, graphic, mechanical, or electronic—without written permission of both publisher and author, except in the case of brief excerpts used in critical articles and reviews. Unauthorized reproduction of any part of this work is illegal and is punishable by law.

Contents

Dedication 7
Acknowledgements 9
Introduction 11

Chapter 1   Decide 35
Chapter 2   Creating Sacred Space 49
Chapter 3   Connect 64
Chapter 4   Setting Intentions & Living Intentionally 77
Chapter 5   Grounding and Centering 95
Chapter 6   Being in the Moment 106
Chapter 7   Release the Past 114
Chapter 8   Envisioning the Future 123
Chapter 9   Trust Yourself – Heart to Heart 129
Chapter 10 Continue Living a Balanced Wellness Lifestyle 136

About the Author 143

Dedication

To my children: Brandon, Jasmine, Julian, Kevin, and Lady J

As I heal, you heal. As we heal, the planet heals. I love you to the moon and back. Thank you for your love and support, even when you weren't quite sure where this was all heading. It means the world to me to see us all healing.

Xoxo
Mom

In loving memory of Lena La Nell Jordan La Ness. Your legacy of love and passion for life live on in the lives you touched. I'm so grateful for your belief in this crazy dream of mine. I love you! You are forever here! Thank you for the quarters. xoxo

Acknowledgements

Thank you to all of the many who have directly influenced my path the last several years:

Katana/Kat Edwards, Erin Lees, Barbara, Tammi Morrison, Sherra Grasser, Richard Seaman, Sarah Christine Nolan, Sama Morningstar, Lauren Dally, Sally Cartensen, Erica Nichole, Monika Thompson, Chandra Brooks, Jennifer Alvarez, Jenny Foertsch, James Van Praagh, Sarah Strizzi

Super huge thank you to my dear friend Shareen Rivera for going above and beyond to help me.

Introduction

From the teachings and activities in this Guide to Balanced Wellness, you can expect new results from new actions. Expect new actions from a new mindset. Expect a new mindset from connecting to your best self and defining your core beliefs. Expect to achieve targeted wellbeing and balanced wellness of spirit, mind, and body when you define your core beliefs and align your mindset and action as a lifestyle. Expect Miracles. And, so it is!"

Are you a highly sensitive person? Do you feel affected by others or by what is going on around you? Imagine this:

Your clothes being tossed around in a washing machine on permanent press.

Swish, swish

Pause.

Swish, swish

Pause

This agitates the items just enough to move them to a new space. Just three to four times of this and the machine has gone full circle, leaving the items headed in whatever direction they were last thrust.

If these items were you, there would be just enough space for a gasp of air to be taken between the surface of the murky sudsy water and the lid.

Imagine now; you are the item in the washing machine. You are underwater and getting tossed around. You are gasping for air, and the only way to get the vital air is to get it yourself. You are desperate; your life depends on it. You must change this situation. Can you feel the need for a vital nutrient missing?

Suddenly, in the moment of extreme need, in your desperation, you realize you are much bigger than the washing machine, and all you have to do is stand up. Stand up on your own two feet and use the strength of both your ego and your essence. As you do, the lid of the machine pops open, and the daylight shines in. You can breathe, there is fresh air filling your lungs and beautiful sunlight hitting your skin. You have hope. You see, there is much more available to you than the dark space you have been drowning in.

Congratulations! By choosing to stand up, you took the stand that was needed by using your own power and energy to get out of the cycle that was tossing you around aimlessly.

If life were a washing machine that cycle of, "Swish, swish, pause," it would be called SURVIVAL MODE.

Do you have a survival mode cycle in your life?

Are you in that cycle now?

Please keep reading dear one, this message with **the steps to shift from surviving to thriving are now in your hands.** It is up to you now to do the necessary work.

Defining your core beliefs, then aligning your mindset and action, is necessary and essential for balanced wellness of spirit, mind, and body. Targeted Wellbeing from balanced wellness is achieved over time as you incorporate the changes you desire into your lifestyle.

At the core, it is simple. Be you. When you are yourself, at the core of your vibe is love. So be love. As you move forward, aligned with love in your core beliefs, mindset, and actions, you will shine brighter and brighter. You have a unique vibe and a unique shine. As you do the work, you will raise the frequency of your vibe/vibration and shine brighter and brighter.

> **Serenity Maven Tip:** *Don't worry if the vibration is a new term. It was for me too. It was easy for me to understand it as the vibe and essence of who I am, without my thoughts and without my body. I'll teach you more about your vibration and frequencies later on in Chapter 2.*

But first, are you ready? Here it comes...

You're invited to be YOU, be LOVE, and SHINE BRIGHT like only you are meant to shine!!!

Usually, we end there. But you've got more ahead of you now. Together we will create a lifestyle where you define your core beliefs and align your mindset and actions so that you can live a lifestyle of balanced wellness. A life with an abundance of peace, joy, happiness, health, wealth, passion, connections, and more!

Now, it's up to you to decide to take steps to show up for yourself, fully, as no one has ever shown up for you. Not even you. It's ok. It's time to be gentle and curious with yourself. Just think who you can be if you show up for yourself full? Can you imagine it? Stop for a moment, imagine you without any limitation of doubt, time, or money. Does this bring you hope?

I remember the day I decided as if it was yesterday. At that moment, I knew I was what needed to change. I had spent a lifetime with my focus on all the things done to me or created by happenstance and circumstance. The mantra I lived by and shared with everyone was, "If it's bad, and it's going to happen, it's going to happen to me." I truly believed this, and I felt I had many good and valid reasons to believe it.

Being born to a single mother in the mid-1970s, I saw the struggle. Yet at the same time, I recall being a happy, carefree, talkative, and mature small child. Looking back, I would say this was only until I was about 6 or 7. Going to school was a turning point for me. I learned was DIFFERENT! I tried so hard to fit in, and it never happened. This rejected child inside me continued to show up for decades. I even tried to parent a family from this space. Somehow I navigated the world of medicine, IT, and Corporate America. I was still trying to fit in, trying to conform to what was expected of me.

Over time the criticisms, rejections, disappointments, and more became too much. It showed up in my life as anything but happy. Everything I measured myself up against, left me constantly feeling like I was not enough. Frustration and anger eventually turned to rage taken. Taken out on those I loved the most. And that was exactly what happened that day, the day I decided that I was what needed to change.

It was me. In order for my family to heal. I needed to heal.

As I stood there, with all my weight on my left foot, so my right hip could be cocked up to hold my 2-year-old daughter on, I was in pain. Physical pain for years, but secretly I was in emotional pain. Or perhaps it wasn't so secret. Those who lash out at others are hurting. I thought I was doing a great job of hiding it day to day, but today it was about to spill up, out, and all over the place in a single moment. It was a moment, at 40 years old when I realized my life was nothing like I thought it would be when we wrote our future selves letters in high school as an assignment and resentments and anger had been building secretly for decades, even unbeknownst to me.

But remembering that day in 2017 is like slow motion now - as I think back to one of the most humiliating times to admit, but back then it was just a flash of moments (Insert the slow-motion voice over here.) "Get the #%!@ out!" I had had it. I had enough of being unheard, disrespected, taken for granted, and taken advantage of. And as those words left my mouth, I time-warped to a memory when the adult child I was yelling at, was a baby and in my arms and I was telling the man in my life to, "Get the #%!@ out!".

I've repeated this scene several times with several relationships. And that is when I realized it in the back of my awareness that I was done. At the forefront, I was still full steam ahead with the unleashing of the wrath. I certainly was not going to have a blow-up and then give in, like many other times. This time I was going to set a firm boundary. He had to leave right then. As I was still being ignored, I got louder. I really lost my shit. This got the message out loud and clear that I wasn't playing around. I felt like I was acting and putting on a show. An internal dialogue going with another dialogue directing the scene. Almost feeling "out of body", or what I now call - disconnected and out of the moment.

It was a familiar happening. And I was done. What I was really done with was done with the repeated cycles that were showing up over and over in my life. In fact, these still continue to show up, but with a new awareness, I am responding and processing differently. Sometimes I'm ready for it and sometimes I'm blindsided and reactive. Yet, still processing and showing up differently.

I realized something different here though. Here in this moment, none of the men who were in my life in the past were here to blame. It was me standing there. It was me who was the common denominator in all the scenarios.

> ***Serenity Maven Note:*** *We can mirror behaviors as a part of surviving. It is not human nature to mimic your surroundings to fit in. However, based on how you were raised (at home, at school, etc.) you may have been taught to conform to fit in with your peers. This type of modification of actions started for me in early childhood with my mother, through my school years with a couple of my teachers and peers, and then continue into adulthood. We can learn to cope in ways that are toxic but acceptable. In order for me to start attracting those who treated me the way I wanted and needed to be treated, I had to believe I was worthy and treat myself with the same expectations - towards myself and others. To do the work to build my confidence, it wasn't and isn't always pretty. But it is freeing. You are worthy. You can set expectations for yourself and you can define your authentic core beliefs. Your future self will thank you for giving yourself the time you deserve.*

As I stood there within feet of the car engine in our family living room (that was never to be there and I had asked for it to be removed repeatedly), next to the futon my son slept on. Taking it in and looking at all of the things everywhere, I had tears streaming, stomach on fire and full of rage.

I've been very black and white in my parenting, focused on principals. We can't get something for nothing or take advantage of others, even if they are offering. At some point, we know the balance is off and we need to stop taking or start giving. If we are not putting in our piece, we cannot expect to reap the rewards.

Within minutes of the explosive interaction, he was gone and so was the thought of a relationship with my son. The son who was on life support for 11 days at 18 months old after being resuscitated during a health crisis. This was not what I dreamed and imagined for him when I was praying for his life in the hospital crib in the NICU. I felt like shit. I felt like a horrible mother. My entire life meaning in this one moment - I failed. I f-ed all my kids up and it was all my fault. Here I was thinking I was loving and kind and I wasn't. I was full of anger and rage.

As the domed ceiling of the grass-roof lake house lit up from the ceiling fan light, from the floor to ceiling windows the darkness from the outside created a dark wall. And like the darkness outside, the darkness and heaviness inside me hit my awareness. Sinking my heart and closing up my throat and tightly shutting my lips. It felt like a ton of bricks falling on me as I swallowed the biggest truth pill around, that it was me.

Years earlier, we sacrificed so much for our safety. Left our mortgaged home, family, friends and almost a career. I was nearly complete with divorcing my estranged husband and in the midst of it, he vanished. Well, not entirely, but had it been before technology it sure would have taken a while to connect the dots and figure it all out. I called his work to reach him. This was around the time cell phones were becoming a regular thing, so it was a bit awkward to call the front desk to speak to him. When the lady answered she said he would no longer be working there. Great, I thought. His ego got the best of him and he quit another job on the spot. She quickly followed up letting me know he would no longer be back. This was the same day a child support order was going into effect. I thought - great, he must be dodging his new payment amount, one he had fought.

Little did I know it was greater and more of a shake-up to our family than that. I remembered a week earlier my co-worker, who was training to become a police dispatcher showed me and my friend how you could look up on the internet people who were arrested and see what they were arrested for. I was still calm, cool, and collected and allowing my mind to wander to some not so far fetched ideas. I call my friend who is still at work and ask her to look him up.

I can hear the shocked terror in her voice. He was arrested and it showed his charges. As she read them to me my hands and legs were shaking uncontrollably. Charged with allegations and facing twenty-five years to life and One Million Dollars bail. I knew the dark side of the man who knew my mental, emotional wounding and how to manipulate me into thinking I was unworthy. This marriage was so explosive, he previously attempted to take my life by strangling me years earlier. I share openly about the effects of staying and going back into a toxic and abusive marriage had and still has on my family in my podcast, Finding Mommy's Soft Voice. But this was beyond those simple and far fetched ideas. This was a life-altering nightmare level. Fear was setting in, my life as I knew it at that moment, forever changed. What was interesting is rather than the terror I had been living with, there was a focused awareness that this was our time to be free and find safety. Yet a deep awareness I was no longer going to have support raising my children.

Serenity Maven Tip: *I knew in my gut that if we did not leave we were not safe. I knew one day he would take my life as he threatened so many times and attempted before if we did not leave. Here is a study provided by the Strangulation Training Institute that supports my fears. "A 2008 study in the Journal of Emergency Medicine suggested that the risks of an attempted homicide increase about sevenfold for women who have been strangled by their partner. The study also found that 43 percent of women murdered in domestic assaults, and 45 percent of victims of attempted murder, had been strangled by a partner in the previous year."*

Source: https://www.strangulationtraininginstitute.com/life-and-death-in-your-hands-strangulation-more-common-in-domestic-abuse-cases/

If you or someone you love are in an abusive relationship there are resources available. You are not alone. Please seek professional help and support.

At that moment I was so overwhelmed I had to surrender to my God of Understanding/Universe/Spirit/Source and ask him to take over. It was just too much for me to comprehend. Luckily I was only minutes away from home and I was able to get my more than trembling, nearly convulsing body home. And then IT kicked into over driver. "IT" being SURVIVAL MODE. I was on a mission to get us to safety. And I did. I stood up. It was time to breathe. To surrender and move forward. Full of fear of the unknown, but also full of hope for a better future for my family I prayed and allowed myself to move forward.

For nearly a decade I was surviving. Dealing with anxiety and getting triggered by the traumatic events of my marriage. I continue to be in this mode as I was raising four children on my own as an independent single mother. Until the beautiful blessing of my fifth.

My youngest daughter has a rare diagnosis of a spectrum that genetically affects the overgrowth of cells throughout the body. Often primarily in one side of the body or specific body parts. It is also notedly often visibly diagnosed by having red birthmarks on the forehead/face and a larger tongue and weight. With this diagnosis comes a higher rate of specific childhood cancers. From the time Lady J was weeks old she began screenings for tumors. At the time it was every six weeks for three years and then quarterly until she is eight. To say my anxiety was triggered was an understatement.

I began to really focus on her and her needs. The needs of the online community we connected with who are also navigating the same diagnosis. As I did, I began to ignore my own needs more and more. I was working for many hours.

I had most of the things I needed growing up. What I did not know and understand, I did not have the nurturing I needed at that spiritual connection level with my Mother. She was emotionally unavailable. In addition, so was her mother when she was growing up. It has been happening for generations in my family. Not intentionally. Homes were full of love. or what was thought of as love, but often toxic behaviors disguised as love. Or when I am honest with the terrifying times, not disguised at love, but straight shit served up in controlling behaviors and or anger and rage.

Most of us, and most likely including you, may be missing that nurturing as well. This set up the blueprint for my relationship and the story I told myself about many of my relationships.

After 8 years, a divorce in process, I was free! Physically free, but not emotionally free from the relationship that had me terrified and operating in fear. So much that for the 5 years, completely safe, I lived in anxiety and constant fear. Unable to trust anything or anyone. Planning for the worst-case scenario and expecting life to be difficult because I was unworthy and deserved all the was happening.

Over time, this unworthiness showed up in ways of pleasing others. Many days that turned into years of doing what others expected I found myself in space of misery, but not yet as my space of being done. At that time I learned about mindset. Boy did I think that was great - and I still do! The mind is powerful and we can reprogram our subconsciousness. However, we have to engage more than just our minds. We have to engage and connect with our authentic selves. The one without the childhood and adult wounding.

I was seeking physical health when I began to be introduced and aware of the tools and steps I share with you in this guide. I now know and understand what these words really mean, "In order for my family to heal. I need to heal." In order to have the deep connections, understanding, love, and respect I was seeking, I had to give it to myself. Accepting, forgiving, allowing the flow of love within me so I can allow myself to move beyond the past of unworthiness I was feeling.

By learning to trust and taking the time to connect to my authentic self, the one beyond the story, I can move forward making intentional choices to create a mindset and take actions that are aligned with my own core beliefs, not defined by others. Starting now, you can do this too by connecting deeply with your authentic self for the answers you have been craving.

What I now know and share with you here is that by connecting to my best self, I could move forward, making intentional choices to create a mindset and take actions that are aligned with my own core beliefs, not defined by others. Starting now, you can do this, too, by connecting deeply with your best self for the answers you have been craving.

Here are the three secrets to living a life full of peace, hope, love, health, and balance. In this Guide to Balanced Wellness, I will break down these three steps and help you create a practice and foundation in your heart and home for living a lifestyle of balanced wellness. By first defining your core beliefs, then second aligning your mindset, and then lastly aligning your actions, you will achieve balanced wellness of body, mind, and spirit. You will be able to create a custom, balanced lifestyle based on your own intuition and knowing.

If I compared my whole life to just one moment, it explained a lot. I was in a rental car in Irvine, California. About a couple of hours into my trip, it hit me. The station I was listening to was in Spanish. Why didn't I notice? I didn't notice because I was so used to putting myself on the back burner. Having a choice of a radio station, or anything else for that matter, wasn't even an option.

I could look at it in several ways. Either as a martyr, angry and resentful or realize that I was exactly where I was doing exactly what I chose to do, on my own. I was states away from home. ALONE. At that time, I would switch back and forth between being a martyr and angry & resentful.

Why was I angry, resentful, frustrated, and at times rageful towards my family? I had allowed life to create me, rather than creating my life. Swish, Swish, Pause. Swish, Swish, Pause. SURVIVAL MODE.

To change, I had to decide to define my core beliefs. If I didn't know who I really was meant to be before all the experiences and exposures came into play, then what was I expecting? If I didn't know what respecting my core values was, how did I create boundaries that communicated respecting my core values?

Can you relate? Are you exhausted from serving everyone else, putting yourself last, and frustrated from not ever being enough? Enough for yourself or others?

In this Guide to Balanced Wellness, I share with you the steps to create the life you may not even be able to dream of right now, or perhaps you have clear visions of where you are going. In either position, you will not be able to:

DEFINE YOUR CORE BELIEFS

First, you must define your core beliefs. Not based on what anyone else has told you, but what you know intuitively. What you know in your gut and heart. The good news is with living in the moment; this is more of a practice than having to sit down with an assignment and create a list.

> **Serenity Maven Tip:** *Pssttt Calling out the Perfectionists take a deep breath. A balanced wellness lifestyle is also about living with intention. Let loose on the rules. Everything is going to be ok.*

CREATE DAILY AFFIRMATIONS

Use daily affirmations that you personally create based on your vision for your life and who you need to be to create that life. Reprogram your mind in alignment with your core beliefs.

LIVE IN THE MOMENT

You are invited to live in the moment. To choose to make decisions in alignment with your core beliefs and aligned mindset.

HEAL YOUR INNER CHILD

Are you reacting or responding to living in the moment? Who are you being when you are not being mindful? Understanding the development of who you be without expectations is one of the most freeing and forgiving experiences I can ever share with you. Helping you understand yourself. Helping you heal yourself. When you heal, your family will heal. As you heal, you can connect at a deeper level to yourself in your own hearth, your own home, and in your community.

CREATE BALANCED WELLNESS

Targeted Wellbeing is a balanced wellness of your spirit, mind, and body through the alignment of your core beliefs, mindset, and actions.

What would you say to life with an abundance of peace, joy, happiness, health, wealth, passion, connections, and more?

Do you say Yes or No? If you say Yes, here are the Serenity Maven Activities created for you in this Guide to Balanced Wellness. You will be guided along your journey through these activities. You will be shown how, but you be left to discover your own, divinely timed awareness.

Serenity Maven Activity #1 - Inventory Time
Serenity Maven Activity #2: Working Through Resistance

Serenity Maven Activity #3 - Connecting to Your Core Authentic Beliefs
Serenity Maven Activity #4 - Getting Real With Yourself
Serenity Maven Activity #5 - Creating Sacred Space At Work
Serenity Maven Activity #6 - Creating Sacred Space At Home
Serenity Maven Activity #7 - Setting Sacred Space Everywhere
Serenity Maven Activity #8 - Creating Sacred Space Now
Serenity Maven Activity #9 - Cutting Cords
Serenity Maven Activity #10 - Your Awareness Level
Serenity Maven Activity #11 - Intentional Living
Serenity Maven Activity #12 - Connected Free Writing
Serenity Maven Activity #13 - Ground and Center
Serenity Maven Activity #14 - Envision Your Future and Best Self
Serenity Maven Activity #15 - Identifying Blocks and Fears
Serenity Maven Activity #16 - The Difference Between Your Intuition and & Your Fears
Serenity Maven Activity #17 - Being Happy, Balanced & Authentic

-----Before you go forward, grab your journal and something to write with----

Serenity Maven Activity #1 - Inventory Time

You're invited to check in with yourself and take inventory at your vibe level, your essence, which is the best version of you. Remember to be gentle and curious.

To do this, place one hand on your heart and one hand on your belly. Close your eyes and take a deep breath; in through your nose and out through your mouth. Nice and slow and controlled. Try it now.

1. One hand on your heart

2. One hand on your belly
3. Close your eyes
4. Breathe - nice slow and controlled cleansing breath, in through your nose and out through your mouth.
5. Allow

Allow anything to come up to your mind that needs to. Don't resist.

Write down what comes up - what it is and the location. It could be goosebumps, pain, twitch, digestive release, any sensation at all. No matter how big or small or how silly or serious it is, there is no wrong answer.

Your truth is not right or wrong; it just is. You have every right to feel yourself and trust yourself. No matter what others have told you, or you have told yourself. Deep breath. Soak that one in, dear one. Is there pain? Tightness? Are you holding stress? Are you feeling hope and flow? After writing what comes up first, then take inventory of your entire body using the table on the next page.

Feel free to include anything you feel, see, hear, think, or just know. Such as words, phrases, symbols, memories, ideas, thoughts. Even if it feels silly. Allow. Don't resist.

Writing Space

Top of Head Physical Feeling:_____ Emotional Feeling:_____

Forehead Physical Feeling:_____ Emotional Feeling:_____

Face Physical Feeling:_____ Emotional Feeling:_____

Throat Physical Feeling:_____ Emotional Feeling:_____

Shoulders Physical Feeling:_____ Emotional Feeling:_____

Chest Physical Feeling:_____ Emotional Feeling:_____

Left Arm Physical Feeling:_____ Emotional Feeling:_____

Left Hand Physical Feeling:_____ Emotional Feeling:_____

Right Arm Physical Feeling:_____ Emotional Feeling:_____

Right Hand Physical Feeling:_____ Emotional Feeling:_____

Upper Back Physical Feeling:_____ Emotional Feeling:_____

Upper Belly Physical Feeling:_____ Emotional Feeling:_____

Middle Back Physical Feeling:_____ Emotional Feeling:_____

Lower Belly Physical Feeling:_____ Emotional Feeling:_____

Lower Back Physical Feeling:_____ Emotional Feeling:_____

Between Legs - Where the front and back of your body meet Physical Feeling:_____

Emotional Feeling:_____

Left Leg Physical Feeling:_____ Emotional Feeling:_____

Left Foot Physical Feeling:_____ Emotional Feeling:_____

Right Leg Physical Feeling:_____ Emotional Feeling:_____

Right Foot Physical Feeling:_____ Emotional Feeling:_____

> ***Serenity Maven Tip:*** *Psssttt. Pssssttt. Yes, you. You may feel some resistance to doing the activities in this Guide to Balanced Wellness, including Activity #1. You may even want to put this guidebook aside now. But where has avoiding and not giving yourself the time you need gotten you? Now take a moment to think of the opposite. What happens when you show up for yourself? Yes, remember, when you show up, great things happen! You've got this!!*

> ***Serenity Maven Tip:*** *You may be thinking, "Don't resist? How do I do that?" If you're like me and have tried to "clear" your thoughts only to have thoughts keep coming, allow the thought, acknowledge it, thank it, release it. This is how to "not resist" what is coming up for you. To work through resistance at any time with anything in your life, or with Activity #1 you're invited to do Activity #2 first.*

Serenity Maven Activity #2 - Working Through Resistance

To allow is to be authentic. To resist, you must have an expectation of what is expected. If you are resisting doing any activity or, do this next activity first and come back. Otherwise, you can choose the order you would like to do Activity #1 and #2. Both create a powerful awareness in your conscious and subconscious mind.

Stop and take a moment to notice how "expectations" feel in your body during this activity. Notice how your authenticity contrasts the resistance.

How expectations feel in my body:

_____

_____

How authenticity feels in my body:

_____

_____

How resistance feels in my body:

_____

_____

You're doing great! Congratulations! You just trusted yourself! And you showed an amazing amount of respect for yourself. Continuing to use these simple steps to this technique, you can define your core beliefs and begin to align your mindset and action in every moment. You've literally just completed ALL 10 steps.

SPEAKING OF ACTION

If you didn't do Activity #1 yet, go back and do it now. If you don't have time, you're invited to go to your phone right now and enter a reminder for when you will work on this next. Tomorrow? Same time?

Remember, new habits create new results. How many times have you missed important things because the action was missing? You're invited to take action NOW. Your future self will thank you! Swish,

swish - pause. Grab that dial on your life and switch it from surviving to thriving and use the tools you already have.

Why am I doing these activities?

As we continue through these activities, you will be taken on a journey of awareness. As this new awareness is applied to your personal experiences & exposures of your own mind, both conscious and subconscious, you will be experiencing changes. What can be referred to as "releasing" the past? This can show up as charges being forgiven (against yourself, others, or others towards you), fears being released, and more.

As a highly sensitive person, you can use the feelings in your body to be authentic. When you use your feelings to define your core beliefs, you can define your authentic self in every moment. This is called LIVING IN THE MOMENT. When you shift to a lifestyle of living in alignment with your core beliefs, balanced wellness of spirit, mind, and body are aligned with your target of wellbeing: Balanced Wellness.

Now that you recognize expectations, authenticity, and resistance, you are invited to add these to your balanced lifestyle toolbox of resources. Let's set the intention now in your subconscious mind to use them. It's time to make a decision. One that could alter the rest of your life.

HERE WE GO!!!!

You are constantly making choices and decisions. Now is no exception. The conscious choice to no longer accept old beliefs handed to you, may be one of the most important decisions you have in front of you to make. This is a conscious decision to stop living the life you have and to start being your authentic self going forward. Your authentic self, meaning the one without the story, the survivor badge, or the mask.

Are you ready to decide and to choose to commit to being, your authentic self by letting go of expectations, hurt, shame, and guilt? Think for a moment. Who could you be without the old stories weighing you down and holding you back?

YES?!!!! AWESOME!!! Great start. Now let's remind you who you are.

You're invited to say this out loud at this very moment and come back to it anytime you need to. Feel free to use it daily if you don't already have a daily mantra or affirmation that you use. You will also be creating your own personal mantras and affirmations in this Guide to Balanced Wellness, which will be even more powerful because it will be very specific to you!!

I am a highly sensitive person, fully supported by my spirit, mind, and body.
I am living in the moment trusting.
I am authentic.
I am worthy of simply being my truth, a living example of my core beliefs.
I am using my awareness to align my mindset with my core beliefs.
I am choosing for my actions to be aligned with my mindset.

I am transforming into my authentic self and releasing the past that no longer serves me through new awareness.
I am gentle.
I am curious.
I am balanced and whole.
I am love.

AND SO IT IS!

Dear one, you've done a lot of work, come back tomorrow and keep going! Talk with you soon!

> ***Serenity Maven Tip:*** *It is essential to support your body, mind, and spirit through using products on your body that are free of toxins, as well as eating whole organic foods, and drinking plenty of water. As you are working through this guidebook, you are moving and releasing old energy (Remember those feelings in your body? Yeah, that is the energy we are talking about.) Taking a shower or a bath is my favorite way to clear the energy from any situation. You can also support yourself by simply washing your hands with water if you are short for time. As a highly sensitive person, you may find that water and nature as essential pieces to your balanced wellness lifestyle.*

Chapter 1

DECIDE

You've decided to choose YOU, dear one. You can give yourself a life better than you have imagined and perhaps dreamed of. Maybe even for the first time, you are simply enough. (Deep breath - envision yourself as enough - and what this feels likes.)

Can you imagine living a life where you are heard, respected, loved, and cherished? Can you imagine your life like this and what it would feel like? No matter how distant from now, allow yourself to pretend at this moment; to daydream and imagine you living your best life. Stop and take a moment to pretend and imagine. Write in your journal things that come up for you.

"What is real or imagined is real to the mind." How powerful of a statement is this for you?

Let me help you break this down. Think of a time you thought you lost something, but then you immediately found it. For just those short moments, did you go through disbelief, disappointment? Possibly even anger, and frustration? Were those emotions real? Yes. Was the situation you were upset about real? No. However, in those moments, it didn't matter. Your body thought the item was lost, so it was reacting as if you lost the item.

Think of another time where you were oblivious to information and positivity kept you in the space of everything being ok. Both times, what was being felt and experienced was not in alignment with reality, but for those moments, your body was responding as if they were reality. When you make a decision, you are choosing what to believe in that moment, and your mind and body will work together in response to your belief.

"Whether You Believe You Can Do a Thing or Not, You Are Right"
- Henry Ford

Serenity Maven Activity #3 - Connecting to Your Core Authentic Beliefs

Here in Serenity Maven Activity #3 I'll help you to further set up your subconscious mind and get in touch with your core beliefs.

Start by placing:

1. One hand on your heart
2. One hand on your belly
3. Close your eyes
4. Breathe - nice slow and controlled cleansing breath, in through your nose and out through your mouth.
5. Allow
6. Continue until you complete 3 cleansing breaths.
7. Allow your belly to expand as you breathe out, focused on every aspect of your breath.
8. Take a moment and show gratitude
    a. to your body for breathing and accepting this vital nutrient
    b. To the universe for providing the air, you are breathing

c. To your God of Understanding, if you have one, for all that is - including the Miracles and blessings.
9. Sit in this gratitude.

Writing what comes up first, then take inventory of your body from head to toe. Be gentle. Be curious. Feel free to include anything you feel, see, hear, think, or just know. Such as words, phrases, symbols, memories, ideas, and thoughts.

Serenity Maven Tips:

- *Even if it feels silly, weird, crazy, dumb, etc. allow what comes up. Don't resist.*
- *Allow yourself 20 minutes for this activity.*
- *Deep healing - If you are doing a deep healing session, allow yourself 1-2 hours.*
- *Play healing music. I like to go to YouTube and search "healing music" to find music that I feel aligned with for the moment.*
- *My favorite place to do these types of activities, aka "the work to heal", is in the bathtub. Nothing feels better than pulling the drain, and all that was shed during the session washes away and down it goes! I just love it!!*
- *You're doing AWESOME!! Remember there are no right or wrong responses during your journey. Just new awareness for you.*
- *Trust that you are always safe, guided, protected and loved. Ask and pray for support during the activities.*

JOURNAL QUESTIONS

Ask yourself these questions and journal on the answers, connected to your best self:

1. What am I choosing to change in my life?
2. What am I choosing to do more of?
3. What am I choosing to do less of?
4. How will this help me with me be my best self?
5. What scares me the most about this change?
6. The support I need from myself to make this change is:
7. The support I need from others to make this change is:
8. What if I don't get the support from others? How will I receive the support I need?
9. What boundaries am I setting for myself?
10. What boundaries am I setting with others?

AFFIRMATION QUESTIONS

Now let's take some of your answers for the above questions and summarize them below. While we will examine some of them again, you will also notice some additional questions. There are reasons for summarizing your response and re-framing them with the new questions. This is giving you another perspective. You will use your Responses for the upcoming Super Sandwich Affirmation Activity.

Questions for Serenity Maven Activity #3	Response (Will be used later in Activity 4)
What am I choosing to change in my life	From above
What am I choosing to do more of?	From above
What am I choosing to do less of?	From above
How will this help me be my best self?	From above
Who do I need to be?	New
How will I respond?	New
How will I feel?	New

As you are writing, if negative things come up as ideas, thoughts, worries, stressors or memories, allow them to come up and say thank you for showing up today. Write down all that comes up to your conscious awareness for yourself. Focus on the feelings, both emotional and physical. You do not need to focus on specific details of what comes up.

You've got this dear one, nothing is more healing than love and gratitude. As you send gratitude, write what comes up in your journal.

> ***Serenity Maven Tip:*** *If you find yourself "looping" back to a memory you choose not to, this a powerful phrase I like to use, "I choose to live in this moment. This memory is now an opportunity for growth at this moment. What expertise have I gained?"*
>
> *"Get the #&$! out of my head! Go away. This thought is not serving my highest good." is also a powerful one. I'm not one to swear often, but WOW!!! TRY IT!! It is SO EMPOWERING!!! And you don't even have to say it out loud.*

All done with Serenity Maven Activity 3? Great job! This was an opportunity for you to see that you do know what it is that needs to be healed, released, and replaced with vibrant and healing self-love, love of the universe, love of your God of Understanding/Universe/Spirit/Source, love of humankind and love of all things capable of loving.

For the next week, come back to and repeat Activity #3 daily. Use your journal. You can follow the questions or allow yourself to free write anything that comes up..

> ***Serenity Maven Tip:*** *If you find that you have missed doing it before going to bed, get in at least 5 minutes. Your time is essential, and some time is better than no time. You'll be happy you did!*

SUPPORTING YOUR JOURNEY

Healing consists of 5 phases:

1. Cleansing: Identify and release emotional blocks
2. Re-energizing. Occurs within 1 week of cleansing
3. Change present life and ancestral patterns
4. Change past life patterns
5. Manifestation in alignment with your highest good

In this Guide to Balanced Wellness, we will be working through the steps to support you for phases 1 through 3 of healing. To intensify the results of your healing journey, you may want to research and learn alternative energy healing practices. Or you may choose to seek out alternative health practitioners to work with.

> ***Serenity Maven Note:*** *The TargetedWellbeingCenter.com's School of Intuitive Healing for personal and professional healing is a resource for alternative healing modalities on your personal or professional healing journey. You're invited to check out the current programs and offerings available.*

"Be the change you wish to see in the world" - Mahatma Gandhi

Serenity Maven Activity #4 - Getting Real With Yourself

will be and how you choose to respond will directly impact the direction you move forward (in some cases, leave you stuck or even moving in a different direction). It's time to get real with yourself, but in doing so, you will be prepared. Your conscious and subconscious mind will already have your intentions known.

In this last activity for this first step, Decide, you are going to create a super-powerful and personal affirmation/mantra. You will be able to use this daily, and any time you feel the need to refocus/align with your decision to create a lifestyle of balanced wellness.

Start by connecting to your best self by placing:

1. One hand on your heart
2. One hand on your belly
3. Close your eyes
4. Breathe - nice slow and controlled cleansing breath, in through your nose and out through your mouth.
5. Allow
6. Continue until you complete 3 cleansing breaths.
7. Allow your belly to expand as you breathe out, focused on every aspect of your breath.
8. Take a moment and show gratitude

    a. to your body for breathing and accepting this vital nutrient
    b. To the universe for providing the air, you are breathing
    c. To your God of Understanding, if you have one, for all that is - including the Miracles and blessings.

9. Sit in this gratitude.
10. Answer the following questions:

What are the ways I have sabotaged myself in the past:

_____

_____

When I ask myself the emotion behind the sabotage it is:

_____

_____

I feel this emotion in my body here:

_____

_____

Write anything else that comes up:

_____

_____

The support I need to make this change:

_____

_____

I am supported by my God of Understanding/Universe/Spirit/Source.

I will support myself by:

_____

_____

I am supported by others:

_____

What if I don't get the support I expect, need, or want? What boundaries am I setting for myself?:

_____

_____

AWESOME REALNESS, DEAR ONE You are doing great! Getting real is being authentic. The level of authenticity you show you are, is the same level of authenticity the world needs from you. No mask, no pretense, no expectations.

Serenity Maven Activity #4 continued: Super Affirmation Sandwich

Use this activity as a guide to create your own powerful affirmation.

1. Response from Activity 3 - Use this space to enter a high level summary description of your responses from activity 3
2. Affirmation - Use this space to create a positive affirmation to support your change. An example is provided and you can tweak it to flow naturally for you. Try to keep the same intent of the affirmation lead shown in the box, but still feel guided to change it.
3. Automatic Negative Thought - As humans we secretly inside feel unworthy and these internal thoughts are. Be honest with yourself as you say each affirmation out loud. (Yes, out loud) so you can hear your "internal self-correction" or automatic negative thoughts. Write whatever it is you feel or hear.
4. Super Affirmation Sandwich - Now look at the automatic negative thought you had for each entry. Go through and

write another positive affirmation which is the opposite of your negative thought.

After filling in the grid, rewrite the affirmation in the space below using the affirmations you wrote in both the Affirmation column and the Super Affirmation Sandwich column.

> ***Serenity Maven Tip:*** *Use an app like Canva to create a beautiful picture with your custom affirmation/mantra on it. Print it and put it up in your home and workspace. Save it as a picture and use it as the background/screensaver for your electronics (phone, pc, tablet, etc.)*

Example:

- ➢ What I am choosing to change in my life?: To be more loving and kind.
- ➢ Affirmation: I am loving and kind.
- ➢ Automatic Negative Thought: I just lost my temper yesterday.
- ➢ Super Sandwich Affirmation: I am patient with myself and others.

If you have any questions with any activity - go to the **Serenity Mavens** group on Facebook or email at: theserenitymaven@gmail.com

Question	Response (Summary from Activity# 3 Grid) *Example:*	Affirmation *Example:*	Automatic Negative Thoughts (ANT) *Example:*	Super Affirmation Sandwich *Example:*
What am I choosing to change in my life	To show up more authentically	I am.. authentic	I hide at times	I am honest with myself and others

What am I choosing to do more of?	Happiness, travel, experiences, friendships, abundance in health and wealth	I have more happiness & friendships than ever. I am healthy and have more money than I need.	I have the world on my shoulders and no support	I am never alone on my journey. I am fully supported by God of Understanding/ Universe/Spirit/ Source
What am I choosing to do less of?	Sadness, loneliness, self-sabotage, limited finances	Sot that I have success and abundance in all things in alignment with my gifts	I am not worthy and I am not perfect	I use the tools and wisdom to align balance and ground when I need to.
How will this help me be my best self?	I have to love myself to love others. Being love is being my best self.	In order to be loving & kind, I allow deep connections as essential.	I've not been so nice in the past	I am committed to my journey and life purpose and will be impeccable with my word
Who do I need to be?	Myself	To do this, I am simply love	I get upset at times of high stress or pressure	I am patient.
How will I respond?	Connecting, acting in alignment with the highest good of all	I choose to respond with compassion & love	I am not always responding. Sometimes I do react on autopilot with old responses and behaviors.	I create safe boundaries in alignment with my truth. I am always healing.
How will I feel?	Free, at peace, alive	I am free & at peace.	I am overwhelmed at times.	I am alive

Example of Final Super Sandwich Affirmation:

I am _authentic. I am honest with myself and others.

I have more *happiness & friendships than ever. I am healthy and have more money than I need. I am never alone on my journey. I am fully supported by God and the Universe.*

So that I *have success and abundance in all things in alignment with my gifts. I use the tools and wisdom to align balance and ground when I need to.*

In order to be *loving & kind, deep connections are essential. I am committed to my journey and life purpose and will be impeccable with my word*

To do this I simply love. *I am patient.*

I choose to respond with *compassion & love. I create safe boundaries in alignment with my truth. I am always healing.*

I am *free & at peace. I am alive.*

I am (same first one) *I am authentic. I am honest with myself and others.*

Write your Final Super Sandwich Affirmation by filling out the grid and then writing the Affirmation and Super Sandwich Affirmation for each entry:

I am _____

I have more _____

So that I _____

In order to be _____

To do this I am _____

I choose to respond with _____

I am _____

I am _____

AND SO IT IS!

AWESOME!! You did it! You are a powerful creator! See how easy it is to trust yourself in a safe space? You have gone through the steps of everything. Now you're going to expand deeper throughout each chapter, as I take you through the journey of discovery, I took myself on (and continue as a lifestyle). You've created the life you have now through consistent action. Imagine your life if that consistent action was in alignment with core beliefs that you define while connecting daily, and as needed to your best self.

As with any lifestyle, the support system you create will help you incorporate the changes and sustain them. In the next chapter, you will expand your safe space beyond you and this guidebook. These sacred places will be the hub for your journey.

Set up a time for yourself on your electronic calendar (smartphone, tablet, pc, etc.) with a reminder to read and do the work for Chapter 2. Give yourself 1 full Hour. Also, include another hour to have some self-care time. That's a total of 2 hours.

See you soon!

Serenity Maven Tip: *No one else will make the time for you. I promise you. If you don't make the time for you, no one will. You are so worthy and so in need of this. Please create the time you need.*

Chapter 2

CREATING SACRED SPACE

The second step to supporting your decision to live an authentic life is to create a space where you can connect with yourself daily. Connecting to yourself daily is essential. It is a new non-negotiable for daily living, even if just for 5 minutes - but ideally a minimum of 20 minutes.

Imagine the waves in the ocean, like the washing machine, moving the ocean's contents with a rhythm of flow. You can either go with the flow or be tossed around, especially when resisting. Release all tension in the body, and you naturally float in water. Fight, and you can drown. When it feels like you are drowning - are you fighting and resisting? When it feels like you are flowing - are you connecting and allowing your life to intentionally flow with the moon cycles?

Moon cycles? Yes! The moon! The moon has a direct relationship with the tides. This invisible force is energy. The moon's energy can be felt in your body. You are highly sensitive and may not even be aware of the time when tension is building most in your life, which may, in fact, be when the full moon. This build-up is natural for release.

Once I started to pay attention, I was really surprised. I was extremely ill with an invisible illness. My monthly cycles started to align with the and my "mood swings" did as well. That how I would best describe it if I needed a two-word label. I would begin to feel rage building, in scenarios that otherwise would not bother me much. As I paid closer attention it was all aligning (My anger and anxiety increasing with my monthly cycles and the full moon. Aligned for releasing all that is no longer serving me.) As I became aware of in my own energy I have begun to shift and manage it. As a highly sensitive person, I did not know what to do to manage my own or how to manage the strong energy I can pick up from others. I was taught to ignore specific parts of my body that intuitively tell us what is aligned with us. I used this space to stuff all my emotions. It was pretty much the "bad" space where I'd put all the negative things to ignore them for time and all eternity, again something I am aware of in retrospect as I have shared my story to help my clients and students.

I had a near-death experience in spring 2017 and had to have a hysterectomy to save my life. My body was no longer creating red blood cells after years of hemorrhaging from a toxic and now recalled medical device. My body was "in the gap" and my body was shutting down. I was not being diagnosed correctly, because, well that takes years to get to that point.

Who takes years to address something so severe? Perhaps a medical mom who is surviving and focused on the life and health of her growing infant over her own.

During the months of this health crisis, I was resting deeper than I ever allowed - well, because I had no choice. My body was DONE. I had to surrender, or my fight would deplete the little bit of energy I had in me. It took nearly a month to get my body to be surgery ready. I was driven by one of my sons across town and taken by wheelchair to get daily infusions. A total of 5 months of iron infusions in a week. It was worth not needing a blood transfusion.

This amazing grass roofed lake house had its downfalls. Only 2 bedrooms and 1 bathroom, located downstairs. To enter the home was another set of stairs. What would seem like nothing and something I can execute

After surgery, I still felt the pain I had before surgery.

I had several womb healing sessions with my womb healer and now Bio-Mystical Womb teacher Sama Morningstar, where Lady J intuitively joined in. As I sat propped against the wall in pain, moving a bit stiff post-surgery, with my legs stretched out wide she sat between my thighs. They were BEAUTIFUL and full of raw emotion, feeling, and awareness. In those sessions, Sama taught me that the trauma was still there. The feelings were still there. I could feel the pain in my removed womb, just as an amputee would still feel a limb that is no longer physically there.

I also learned about where to feel and how to use my feminine power. Opposite of what I was taught growing up. Growing up any feelings in this area was "bad". I knew I would be a student under her teachings after those sessions.

It was during one of her healing workshops where we used guttural sounds and body movements that momentously transformed my life and the life of my family. During my session my family got sick to their stomachs and were throwing up. The next morning, I woke up and did the same. To my surprise, the pain was gone.

It came back briefly at those deep levels at one point when I had emotionally abusive contact with someone from my past. This confirmed for me how my emotional pain was being expressed in my physical body. I then did more work through steps to release that trauma.

After 2 years of listening and trusting my power and connectedness, instead of calling my feminine power bad - I'm using it and my life is coming together - closer and closer to my vision.

I still get hormonal and I can check the moon. Doing the work to release the energy through meditation and energy work had been life-changing for the support of aligning body, mind, and spirit for my clients and me. As well as many others I have met through sharing my intuitively guided moon meditations. This has been so powerful I am entering a 13-moon cycle apprenticeship for Bio-Mystical Womb Healing under Sama through the Womb Centered Healing Temple.

As you can see it is a process. It's been 2 years between personal sessions and entering the apprenticeship. Following my heart and intuition. Transforming and entering a space where I am ready to learn more of an area of healing, I am drawn to with moon energy.

Bringing your awareness to the energetic flow of the universe, including the moon and sun will support you - whether in the process transformation or maintaining a balanced lifestyle. As your awareness is now recognizing things that are not in alignment with the flow - they are out of balance. Some people will say this is no longer aligned with you, or is not vibing with you, this means it is a low vibe. As part of living your lifestyle of balance, harnessing the moon energy as part of your lifestyle will catapult your healing journey.

> **Serenity Maven Tip:** *You want a science lesson? Google is your friend. I know that the perfectionist mind must fill all the holes. You must research and challenge what is being said to believe it. I get it! Me too! I was there, even almost a year into my journey, while helping others.*

Soon you'll be in the space of trusting yourself, and when that happens, the freedom from no longer having to prove yourself and challenge others. Can you imagine it? Allowing yourself to relax and put your armor down? I should feel like flow. Flow just like the waves, beautifully and naturally going out and coming back, affecting the overall tides and timing.

This happens based on many factors, including the Moon's force/energy.

Force is energy. The moon's energy has a direct relationship to the tides. This body of water is massive and is controlled by the moon. How much water are you made up of? What effect does the moon's energy have on human beings?

Now, let's think about this. When are the busiest nights for First Responders, Police Stations, and Emergency Rooms? On a Full Moon. All of us are affected by the moon's energy, regardless if you are aware of it or not. Therefore, you might as well harness and intentionally use it.

Sun Energy - Sun energy also affects the tides. It is energizing and enriching to the body, mind, and spirit.

What has energy? Everything has energy. Energy has a frequency that can be measured. Such as with music or other sounds. This frequency is a vibration, or what you may already refer to as a "vibe," short for vibration.

The frequency at which energy vibrates will determine if something is a high vibe or low vibe. Positive is high vibe and negative is a low vibe. The highest and most positive frequency is LOVE. Love heals all things. Raise the frequency and vibe,

Energy attracts like energy. When I do the work to raise my vibe and set the intention

Have you used the word vibe or energy without realizing it? Based on how you use them, do you already have a belief in energy? Such as,

"High vibes"
"Positive Vibes"
"The vibe here is off."
"The energy in here is off."
"I'm not vibing with this"
"He/She sucked the energy out of the room."

What is a sacred space? Sacred space is an area you create that is a high vibe. Creating sacred space is necessary at all 3 levels of spirit, mind, and body.

As a highly sensitive person, do you claim that how you feel is a result of your environment, who you are with, and what you are doing? If you are not intentionally setting sacred space as you go about your day, you are most likely easily affected by those around you. Let's talk about how you set sacred space.

This first thing is awareness. Without the acknowledgment of how sensitive you are and tools to protect yourself, you are probably not aware of how much of the vibes around you, that you are picking up.

These are the steps I use to set sacred space:

- Set the intention to have low vibe energy leave
- I say out loud or in my head, "Only the energy of the highest healing light and love may remain, all other energy must leave now."

- If going into a low vibe space, I will do this upon entry
- Sometimes I notice it late, upon my awareness, I take action - without judgment. As a former perfectionist, it can be easy to go into a space of self-shaming for not being "aware" sooner. You're invited to be gentle and curious in these moments.

Where to set sacred space:

For your spirit, mind and body: everything has its own energy and that energy can be directed or transferred from one item to another. Creating a physical, emotional, and spiritual sacred space is important. Most important is that is clear from clutter and toxic exposures. You can add things you love into this sacred space.

Being a Mom of 5 in a 2-bedroom house with 1 bathroom, there wasn't much space for me to call my own. I claimed the bathtub as my sacred space in the home.

Record Ssccrraacth zrrrrrrrrrt! Wait, the 1-single bathroom? How did I do that? I made myself a priority. I realized as the head of a toxic household, I had to be the most toxic. A John Maxwell quote I've heard over and over in my head, "An organization is run from the top down. No matter how great the workers are, they cannot rise above the leader." Home is the same way.

So yes, with a great commitment to healing myself and my family, I committed to an hour of meditation and healing every day for 3 months. Applying the logic that 20 minutes of meditation is at least 60 minutes of restful sleep. My house would start to stir around 5:30 to 6:00 am. And YES, I would be out of the tub by then.

Every morning, with great anticipation, I would gather all my "stuff." Journal, candles, essential oil, Epsom salt, sage, and crystals into the bathroom to fill the tub with hot water to soak while I did my self-care time. I started to call it Lotus Reiki. As I sat in the water to grow, the dirt of my life was fertilizer for my roots. Each time I drained the water, I would imagine all the negative energy washing away. I cannot express into words how amazingly freeing this is.

Balanced Wellness/Targeted Wellbeing

In a moment, you will define what sacred space means to you. Spiritually, mentally, and physically, to support how you feel, what you think, and what you do. As you continue to bring sacred space into your everyday lifestyle, you will be defining your core beliefs and doing the work to align your mindset, such as affirmations and setting intentions. Most importantly, giving yourself the time to create a plan of action creates an overall lifestyle in alignment with your core beliefs and mindset. Balanced wellness of body, mind, and spirit is achieved through the alignment of your core beliefs, mindset, and actions. This balance of wellness is the target for complete wellbeing.

Today, I still have my morning self-care routine before the house stirs. My me time is essential. Your 'you-time' is essential. "Fill from your saucer, not your cup." Lisa Nichols

What does your daily selfcare routine look like?

_____

_____

Which of the following do you feel drawn to (can be all! Or add your own!):

Self/Spirit
Prayer

Meditation
Journaling
Affirmations
Environment
Candles
Sage
Incense
Essential Oils
Crystals
Reiki Healing
Angel Messages

Hydration Support/Flushing/TRIFECTA
Detoxing of Spirit, Mind, & Body
Water
Herbal Tea
Organic Fruits
Organic Vegetables
Clean Eating

Specific for Women - Womb Centered Healing
Vaginal Steaming
Yoni Eggs

Other _____

> ***Serenity Maven Tip*** - *Let's face it, you are already waking up around 3 am and mindlessly scroll Facebook from all the stress. Can we just rename stress to un-aligned? Looking back, I was so unaligned I couldn't sleep well. Are you unaligned? Sacred space is essential for creating and living a life that is aligned with your best self and life purpose.*

Setting sacred space can be amplified with alternative practices, such as Reiki. Reiki is universal life energy and vibrates at the highest frequency, which is love. Love of your God of Understanding/Universe/Spirit/Source. Love, being the highest, positive, most healing energy. With Reiki, the intention is everything. There is no perfection, but there are Miracles! When I discovered this, I became a Reiki Master Teacher. This means I have gone through all three cycles of Reiki teaching and detoxing.

Reiki Level 1 - the ability to heal yourself, others, pets, and plants using hands-on techniques

Reiki Level 2 - the emotional self-journey and sending distance reiki healing energy

Reiki Master - mastery of connection to your God of Understanding/Universe/Spirit/Source

Reiki Teacher - teaching and attuning others with all three levels of reiki and teaching, techniques, principles and healing integrity.

Reiki is just one healing modality that uses energy. Reiki will take you through a journey of healing and self-discovery. It is recognized by western medicine as a complementary or alternative health treatment. Kaiser Permanente, a leading healthcare provider. (feel free to google "Kaiser reiki."

It is also recognized by the US government, as Reiki treatments are covered under the HSA - Health Savings Account & FSA - Flexible Spending Accounts, when prescribed by a physician.

Another is EERT, an energetic emotional release technique. EERT is used to clear energetic blocks tied to vibes that need to be released.

These can be both low vibe and high vibe energies. Let's just say I was shocked when I had Joy to release! But is also explained why I burst into tears when I am joyful. I had an overabundance of joy stuck as an emotion. When that emotion was triggered, it was over the top. Same with low vibe energies. Such as abandonment, anger, resentments, criticisms, judgments, and more.

If you are easily triggered and don't want to talk to anyone about your shit, EERT and Self Reiki are what I would recommend. You can see others, but if you're like me and need some deep, deep healing, I would also recommend you learn these two healing modalities to practice on yourself.

At $75-$150 for an hour reiki session, 365 days a year, you save $27,375 - $54,750. If you were given the opportunity to heal yourself and save this much, would you do it? If YES, go into your smartphone now, and set an appointment to learn about ANY healing modality that will help you on your journey to freedom with a balanced lifestyle. And let's face it. If you're not willing to take action. Self-sabotage is at play here.

Ask yourself, how does self-sabotage show up for me?

_____

Where is it showing up in my life now?

_____

When being real with myself, in order to have what I want and dream of, I must stop _____. If not, I will keep ending up in the same place over and over.

I AM READY, and so it is.

Set an appointment with yourself. [ ] Check when done.

> ***Serenity Maven Tip:*** *This is also an opportunity to follow your intuition. What lights you up is meant for you. If it sparks interest for you, keep looking deeper into it.*

Serenity Maven Activity #5 - Creating Sacred Space at Work

As you navigate the day, you can create sacred space as you go. If you work in a public setting or office space, bringing in personal items may not be an option. Don't worry! Sacred space can be as small as an imaginary bubble of energetic protection around you, or you can clear the energy of the entire space/building. Especially spaces you share with others. If necessary, go outside or to your car if those are options. In today's day and age, technology allows for telecommuting. Due to their being no limit to the time and space that energy can travel, don't be fooled. Even for someone who telecommutes, setting sacred space is essential.

***Serenity Maven Activity #6* - Creating Sacred Space at Home**

Locate a space that you can use to feel a sense of calm. It could be anywhere in your home. Inside or outside. If you have a large family or limited space, be open to accepting out of the box spaces. For me, my bathtub was the best and quickest way to start. I've gone from having formal spaces for a sanctuary to simply just turning on the bathtub and climbing in. I raise the vibe crystals, essential oils, smudging sticks high vibe must, and often candles. Close your eyes now.

What do you envision as your ideal space?

_____

_____

Great! Allow that to come to you. AND SO IT IS!

What do you envision as the space you can use in this very moment, without it being perfect?

_____

_____

I will use this space for the very first time

_____

_____

_____

Enter a reminder on your phone to do use your sacred space for the first time. As well as ongoing/daily if you need accountability. This is not a reminder to build up shame if you miss it. But an opportunity to create a reminder for what is important to you. It may take time to work through the old self-sabotaging behaviors, but in time it will happen. Different areas of your life will begin to shift and transform, including consistently making yourself a priority.

Serenity Maven Activity #7 - Setting Sacred Space Everywhere.

No matter where you go, you can create a sacred space. If you tend to stay away from crowds or going into public because of being overwhelmed or it just being too much for you, setting sacred space as you navigate the world will open up doors and opportunities of connections that you crave. As a human being, you are meant to be connected to others. Any isolation or avoidance was an old way of coping. Using all the steps I teach you in this Guide to Balanced

Wellness, including sacred space, those connections will become greater and richer. You will call in your tribe. You will begin to feel safer and safer, being your authentic self. One who shines your light brightly to show others.

> ***Serenity Maven Tip****: Yes, remember those prayers. Where you wanted to be shown your purpose and be someone you were destined to be, but the shame and guilt from experiencing trauma. Or if you want to get very REAL, the shame and guilt from creating trauma? This is it.*

You are meant to be you. Which is simply love. And as you allow your authentic light of love to shine, you will be living your purpose. No matter what that looks like.

As you transform to align with your authentic core beliefs, there will be resistance. Let's get real. I've had resistance, even writing this chapter. I felt unworthy of telling others how to create sacred space because I am not the best housekeeper. This is where my own limiting beliefs and the old sabotaging story came sneaking back in. I share this openly with you because 2 ½ years of mindfully being aware of aligning my spirit, mind, and body, I still have to use my tools. I will always have to use my tools. This is why it is a lifestyle. A way of being. I don't just tell you something I heard. I share with you what I do to live a life - not free of anxiety and triggers, but one where I can manage them through awareness and honoring what my spirit, mind, and body need.

While I am not the best housekeeper, I do have sacred space in my home. Even if on some days it is only the bathtub or an invisible bubble around me. Do not allow perfection or shame to keep you from honoring the steps you are taking. In time, all with come together.

Let's face it. You've been through a lot in your life. You've come a long way. You're exactly where you need to be right now. And you will continue to be. xoxo

Serenity Maven Activity #8 - Creating Sacred Space Now

Decide where your sacred space will be for today and this week. The sanctuary you may be imagining, it will come. It's important to you, and it will happen. But for now, this is an opportunity for you to accept as is, without expectation of what your sacred space will look like. It's an opportunity for you to decide what your sacred space will feel like and to create that sacred space now, through your state of being.

Allow that. Breathe in and imagine what your sacred space FEELS like. Congratulations. You JUST DID IT! You created a sacred space by simply setting the intention and taking action.

You are in more control of your situation, despite your circumstances. I hope, through this chapter, you have found a sense of release of expectations and fears of having to be perfect. You are enough. Your intentions are enough. Your thoughts are enough. Your actions are enough. As you give yourself the time to connect daily, this will become more and more clear. As you connect daily, you'll be able to define your core beliefs for yourself in a sacred space. As align your mindset and action, you create a lifestyle of balance through this connection. Freedom from this state of targeted wellbeing is in your hands, dear one. Can you FEEL IT?

Chapter 3

CONNECT

Dear one, this chapter may be one of the most important chapters you read in your life. Connecting to your best self, your God of Understanding/Universe/Spirit/Source and others (or disconnecting from others) is essential to define your authentic core beliefs. In chapter 2, we just learned about setting sacred space. Whenever you connect, you want to be sure you have set sacred space. While we are talking about this as an activity right now, over time of doing it daily and as needed throughout the day, connecting becomes connected and a way of being.

The breath is the key to connecting. Breath is something so simple, yet so complex. Without it, you are nothing. With it, you are living. Intentionally using your breath to reset and balance is the most powerful tool in your **Serenity Maven Tool Box**. If you are not using your breath as a tool, you will have the chance to try it shortly, as we go through a Serenity Maven Activity together. Whether or not you are using your breath consciously, you are invited to set the intention now to be aware of your breath and reminded of its importance, when needed.

Think about it. When you are under stress, what does your body do to naturally release? You sigh. You may even grumble some guttural sounds. What would happen if you took an intentionally focused breath in these moments? What would happen if you were so self-centered and grounded you could feel when you are not aligned? What would happen if you proactively stopped and took a breath BEFORE going into situations you know are stressful?

Yes! Imagine that? Using the resetting tool of breath BEFORE you do something. What would being connected look and feel like? How is that different than how you're living and being now? When we do things consciously, connected, we are intentionally living in the moment. We'll go over intention more in another chapter. But as you can see, each chapter dives in deep to help you consciously and subconsciously master each area. Mastering the use of connecting and breath will take time. If you forget, instead of getting down on yourself for forgetting. Dear one, this is your opportunity to get excited that you remembered! This is a gem opportunity for awareness. If you want to change, you will need to stop in these moments and send love to yourself. With an open mind, open heart, curiosity and gentleness

> ***Serenity Maven Tip*** *Pssstt pssst - Did you catch that? Did you see what we just did? We just went into the opposite land. A place is different than what you were taught. Every single person has what is called Automatic Negative Thoughts (ANTs). As you become more and more aligned with your self-centered authentic self, your ANTs will begin to stand out. Some more than others. Stopping in these Gem opportunities of awareness to ask your best self, "What is it that I need to know about this? What awareness about myself am I learning? What am I ready to shift and up level from this experience, if anything?*

Considering I already said connecting is one of the most important tools, dear one, let's dive in further!

Your breath is your body's "On-Off Reset Button". When you take a focused breath, you are affecting all the chemicals in your amazing vessel of your being. Instantly. For fight or flight mode, breath is the way to relax. If you have experienced trauma, fight, or flight can easily be triggered.

Before I ever connected and intentionally used my breath, I would go try to think my way logically through everything. At times, I would be triggered by severe trauma, and I would get flashbacks, and I had a hard time shutting off the looping thoughts and images. To counteract this, I would go start repeating random, unrelated/off-the-wall words until my mind would forget about the memories. If often would feel shame and guilt, wondering if others knew the obsessive thoughts looping in my mind. What I didn't realize, while this helped me get it out of my conscious thoughts, it was not really serving me to heal. It was simply not making me feel bad at a conscious level.

What I have discovered through my experiences, which aligns with what I've been taught, is that being in the present moment is a way of being and living, and this connection or awareness is essential. You've probably heard this one, or maybe you haven't, but here it goes, my version, "When you are stuck in the past, this can make you feel depressed feelings. When you are stuck in the future, this can have you feeling anxiousness. When you are focused, aligned, self-centered, and grounded, you are living in the moment with a flow and ease and are ready to hear and feel your own intuition. This state of being is what we call Living in the moment."

Unfortunately, most of us are not taught how to do connect or reset with our breath but may be familiar with the concept. You may have been told or even told others to stop, take a deep breath. Or Stop and breathe during times of distress. I can hear these familiar phrases now in my own head, yet I never really knew why or what I could and SHOULD use my own breath as a tool.

> ***Serenity Maven Tip:*** *Are there other phrases throughout different aspects of your life that you hear or use in this same way? Where perhaps the meaning is more significant than you ever really explored?*

Breath is used to connect with your best self, your God of Understanding/Universe/Spirit/Source and others. If you are not connected and aligned, breath is used to reset.

When we are focused on breath - we are living and being in the moment. If you find yourself feeling worry, stress, sad, and/or anxiousness, you are not being in the moment. By focusing on your breath, you can bring yourself to the present moment, helping to release your focus on the past or the future.

Let's do try this together now. I like to close my eyes to help me focus and remove the distractions of the space I am in. You are invited to do the same.

Sit up straight. Your posture and physical alignment will enhance how you feel about the alignment of your vibe. If you can, sit up straight. If you are lying down, become aware of your body and straighten as much a possible. As you do, show gratitude for the ability of any movement you can make. You can take your focus on this gratitude down to the movement of your eyes read this or the movement of your eardrums to listen if hearing this read to you.

Sit with this gratitude for a moment. As you do, begin to focus on your breath, entering your nose. What does it sound like? What does it feel like? What does it smell like? What temperature is it? Are you allowing your belly to expand as your breath expands, or are you holding yourself based on expectations?

Imagine your breath traveling and entering your bloodstream to supply needed nutrients to all the cells of your body.

You just used your breath to connect with yourself, as you have in other chapters. However, this time, it was different than the prior Serenity Moments. You were focused on only one aspect of every moment that passed, your breath.

Write down how you felt when taking the breath.

How do you feel now?

How is this different than before focusing on your breath?

Now that you are all about breath and how to use it. Let's talk about ways you can use your breath consciously and proactively or when you are enlightened with that gem opportunity of awareness that breath will help you.

Uses for focused breath to feel centered:

- To start your day
- When praying
- During meditation and self-care sessions
- When making decisions
- When feeling stressed
- Before going into stressful environments & situations
- You begin to feel anxious

- You realize you are anxious
- You have physical pain
- You have emotional pain
- To end your day
- Anytime you have a gem opportunity of awareness

Serenity Maven Tip - You can magnify the power of your breath. When focused on your breath, close your eyes, and allow yourself to feel gratitude. Sending gratitude to all your cells. Gratitude is one of the quickest ways to raise your vibe.

I will never forget when I started this journey. It was hard for me to find anything I was grateful for, let alone quiet my mind and clear my racing thoughts. In time, that changed to looking forward to quiet moments alone. Clear in thoughts so I can hear amazing intuitive messages from within and from the universe and my God of understanding. Doing this daily, it only took several weeks, and I was able to look back over the same time period and find so much to be grateful for. If this is an area of struggle, you're invited to simply show gratitude for having your breath support you, without conscious effort. No matter what, it is there to support you and show you constant support. And it will, for the rest of your life.

The struggle is real...

What if you are struggling with coming into the present moment, even when focused on your breath? Is there anything you can do to support yourself further? Yes! Yes! Yes!

First, don't fight the negative thoughts. Allow them but listen to them. What is important about that thought? Is it something you must be honest with yourself about and need to take honest action that your soul has been crying out for you to do? Perhaps there is an obligation you feel tied to. Maybe even an expectation is given to you from your childhood and upbringing?

Let's look at this example: Another frustrating experience at your JOB (perhaps at a job you never really imagined yourself doing, but have been at for years or even decades? You can't get it out of your head. That THING that happened. Replaying the incident over and over. Perhaps even saying what you REALLY wanted to say. Stuck on loop. Instead of daydreaming about all you desire, you catch yourself rehashing over and over in your head how things should have gone. And if you're a lot like the old, surviving me, you go into being overly critical of yourself, your words, your actions. Maybe even leading to shame, guilt, or embarrassment for your own behaviors. This stays with you all day, maybe even all night, keeping you awake or preventing you from getting that rested sleep you crave. It may even stay with you weeks, months, or years depending on what it is. But this time, you decided to be intentional, and use your breath to focus, ground, and center yourself.

You go to your sacred space. You close your eyes. You breathe. But you just can't drop it from your mind. Go ahead and focus on the worry. Say thank you to your best self for allowing you to be aware of the things that need to shift or change. Ask yourself, what is it you need to know about this worry. Place one hand on your heart and on hand on your belly as you do this. It will help connect to your deep wisdom and your heart space.

Here is a very important part,

LISTEN. Listen and trust.

Listen to what you hear. No matter how silly or far off from what you logically think or have thought. Ask yourself, "What action do I need to take to help release this situation?"

Again, LISTEN.

Think back to all the times you have regrets. Was it when you didn't listen or listened but didn't take action? Yes? Me too! Even the times where I was hurt by others. I was warned. I ignored the signals in my body, just like I was raised too. I was raised in a home where things were "off". Where I realize now, I was not nurtured at the levels I needed to be. Especially emotionally.

Serenity Maven Gift: Be sure to do the 8 Day Chakra Challenge offered at the end of this guidebook. It will help you with inner child healing to further shift from surviving to thriving. You will use the tools in this guidebook throughout that challenge. Some of my clients start the challenge without any clue of these tools you are learning, so don't feel like you have to finish this guidebook right now if you are feeling drawn to find out more about the challenge or to dive right into it. Access to the challenge is a gifted bonus to you for saying YES to taking the action needed to shift and transform from surviving to thriving. Please honor yourself by allowing yourself to receive this great wisdom.

TAKE ACTION

Yes, this time, despite your fears, it is time to take action. I can hear my dear friend, financial coach Jenny Foertsch, now. I can hear her quoting Thomas Jefferson, "If you want something you've never had. You must be willing to do something you've never done."

Even if that action is simply writing down your thoughts. It takes only 5 seconds for a thought of genius to go away, even after daydreaming about it for 30 minutes. I like to set the intention to be lead to read the note at the right time. And guess what? As silly as it sounds - it works!!

> ***Serenity Maven Tip:*** *Each time you hear something for you, write it down. Set the intention to come back to this in the future when needed, too. Ask your spirit team to help you with the divine timing of taking action. It could be hours, days, months or even years from now. Regardless, receive the message now and write it down. Some call this a "hit", "download", "message," "message from your God of Understanding/Universe/Spirit/Source" or other terms. You may even have your own term.*

But the key is to take action. When your action is consistently (not perfectly) aligned with your core beliefs and mindset, you will feel the shift from surviving to thriving. Thriving is a state of being. Your authentic action is not only required, but it is also essential to thrive, no matter what is going on around you.

ACTION QUOTES.

Ohhh Quotes, I love them. So inspiring Yup, taking a little deep dive in our deep dive. Trust me, you're going to need them in a few. I'm going to be pushing you to stretch past your comfort zone. So let's prime the pump now and soak these up!

What are others I influencers saying?

If you want something you never had. You must be willing to do something you've never done. **Thomas Jefferson**

Not making a choice is a choice. **Unknown**

"The great courageous act that we must all do, is to have the courage to step out of our history and past so that we can live our dreams." **Oprah Winfrey**

"Whatever relationships you have attracted in your life at this moment, are precisely the ones you need in your life at this moment." **Deepak Chopra**

"Authenticity is a collection of choices that we have to make every day." **Brene Brown**

"When we fulfill our function, which is to truly love ourselves and share love with others, then true happiness sets in." – **Gabrielle Bernstein**

Ready to be stretched?

Now, if you've never done work with energy, something you cannot physically see, this may be a stretch for you. It certainly was for me. But I was still drawn to learning. I use this tool when I find mind self stuck in distracting thoughts about a specific situation or person. If I don't use it sooner than later, I can simply get to a space of overwhelm. Feeling physically pulled in multiple directions. But if you're willing to pretend with me, try it, and see for yourself how you feel after, this could be one of the most freeing tools in your Serenity Maven toolbox.

Using your breath to come into the present moment, you are able to connect with your highest most authentic version of yourself (aka your best self), your God of Understanding/Universe/Spirit/Source, and the highest most authentic version of others. You can also use this awareness in the present moment to recognize and disconnect from low vibe connections. These connections are called cords. Imagine a cord or rope connecting you/attaching you to someone or something. There are often labels used here, such as co-dependency, but we are staying away from labels. I share this with you because you may be very well versed in co-dependency. However, this is taking it from what we logically know to what it feels like in your body. By doing this, you will be able to recognize how you react or respond physically, emotionally, and as part of your vibe and essence. Reacting is part of surviving. Responding is a way of showing up for yourself and others.

Ready to try cord-cutting to disconnect from low vibe (aka toxic) connections?

Here we go again. I know, something that may be new. If the sound of cutting cords feels weird - ok. If this feels different - ok. If it feels scary - ok. If you are freaking out about trying something new, here is a gem opportunity for awareness for you! A perfect time to try out some of the things you have learned! YAY!! You get to try things out!

Serenity Maven Activity #9 - Cutting Cords

Your assignment for this chapter is to do a cutting cords meditation and repeat as often as you feel drawn too. You can either guide yourself through this if you already know how to. Or you can simply use the one available in the Serenity Maven Meditation Library.

To get your access to the meditation library go to:

http://bit.ly/serenitymaventoolbox

Check in about the cord-cutting.

Remember to listen only to love. Your intuition always speaks lovingly, even when it is bold and warning of danger. Place one hand on your heart, one hand on your belly. Close your eyes. Take three nice slow cleansing breaths. In through your nose and out through your mouth. Allowing your belly to expand as it needs to. If stresses or worries come up. Honor them. Show gratitude and dismiss them. As you are focused, check in with your best self and ask yourself, "Is cord-cutting in alignment with my highest good? What is it I am fearing? Where is this fear coming from? As I replace fear with love, I step into freedom."

> **Serenity Maven Tip:** *You can cut cords with anything. A new job, a move, a relationship, and more!*

Now that you are connected to your best self - you can begin the cord-cutting meditation.

I like to pretend my fingers are scissors and imagine an invisible connection being cut. There are many ways to do this. If you have your own way, feel free to use that or be open to trusting you know what you need to do to cut cords and just do it intuitively. If you're still an entry-level, just take a deep breath, relax, and keep reading.

What an amazing and powerful gift breath is. It not only resets but allows you to connect to the highest version of yourself and others. You're invited now to set the intention to have an awareness of your tools as you need them, including cutting cords.

Before I cut cords, I check to see if it feels like I am the one attaching or if the other is the one attaching. When I first started, I noticed that having the connections was so familiar it often felt comfortable to leave the cords in place. This was an old way of being that kept me stuck, but the awareness that I was allowing and often seeking the toxic connections was a painful awareness I had to work through. Depending on the situation, the cord-cutting may need to be multiple times.

We've mentioned intention several times now, let's talk more about that in the next chapter.

Chapter 4

SETTING INTENTIONS & LIVING INTENTIONALLY

Intention is everything and the basis of everything I live by and teach, which if you notice, this is the longest chapter. But don't worry, as much as I have to share, this chapter teaches you about how "easy" it can be. Well, compared to the hard way. Before we continue, let me share with you that I'm about to expose you to the "Why Kid" inside me. The one who drove my parents crazy, with question after question to understand. But bringing you on this little adventure with me is to show you the contrast with the rest of this entire book. The difference between THINKING and ANALYZING vs. CONNECTING and TRUSTING your way through life. For nearly the first 40 years of my life, I did anything but trust.

Dear one, I've been breaking down terms for you in each chapter, so you can take the essential actions to create "Balanced Wellness." For this chapter, the term Intention stumped me for a second. It's certainly a word that has been rolling off my tongue for a couple of years. I'm sitting here questioning if I am even using it correctly as a real word? Or is this a "Woo Woo" term I picked up on my journey?

Well now let's see! Am I using it "correctly" In proper 21st-century form, I just googled the word 'Intention', a word I use often as a verb?

(Pssst pssst. If you're like me and English isn't your thing from school, a verb is an action. And yes, you can be the kid with red marks all over your page and still become an author. That's what the editor is for! It's amazing the lies we tell ourselves that hold us back. Isn't it?)

Wow! Ok! Get this?!? Little to my surprise. Intention is listed as a noun. A noun, according to the dictionary, is "a word (other than a pronoun) used to identify any of a class of people, places, or things (*common noun*), or to name a particular one of these (*proper noun*)."

Ok! This reference is definitely NOT an action. So, where does the term "Setting Intentions" come from? Distracted a bit, I'm wondering how I use a noun as a verb. I just googled the word "verb" just to be sure I remember what I learned more than three decades ago. And yet another surprise!

The actual word "verb" is both a noun and a verb. Any by taking the word Intention and using it as an action, we are simply verbing a noun.

Do you have a headache yet? Yeah, me too! Do you remember what intention means? Yeah, I was distracted by all the logical thinking I didn't even share it with you. How often do distractions keep you from SEEING or HEARING your own point?

1 - a thing intended; an aim or plan

And

2 - the healing process of a wound

The intention that I teach and live by, as part of living a balanced lifestyle, is a combination of these two. And I never even realized #2 was part of the definition, heck, just a bit ago I was googling if it was even a REAL word? LOL!

How cool is this? It just occurred to me, through my own experiences of healing, that we can focus the vision, and as we move forward, we are also healing wounds. Through the intentional movement and shift, the healing happens. The healing is in the journey. If you are worried about not being enough or knowing enough, it's time to release that.

You can no longer accept waking up and doing the same thing over and over, just because. You were meant for more. As you intentionally live, you are experiencing the healing process of a wound. Committing fully to the process includes allowing yourself to dictate the pace at which you go. At any point in time, you can ask to speed up, slow down, or take a break. Your intention is everything. Your intentions are a powerful aspect of your creating and manifesting.

As I think back to all the stressful jargon as this chapter started, it had me feeling a bit anxious in the chest. Wow, that was a lot to digest and comprehend. I realize as I go into thinking mode, I immediately shift to how do I do it perfectly? What is the correct way? The stress of it all is almost paralyzing. Even making it more difficult to simply breathe. It feels a bit suffocating to try and follow along and read the above message.

While this is just a fun play on words, it is complex to digest. I've gone down the rabbit hole of the technology realm, Professor Google. This activity reminds me a bit of how I USED to digest my own life, with all the chaos happening around. It was too exhaustive to digest and comprehend. Allowing distractions to keep me from moving forward. I was really comfortable in this space.

Again, this is an example of how INTENSE I would thing through EVERYTHING. It was EXHAUSTING, to say the least. But perhaps you too understand this NEED to be accepted and loved. This need to be perfect. Through your exposures and experiences, you have created a relationship template. Starting from the time you were conceived.

Through my own relationship template/model, I was pressured to be ready and prepared at all times. This grew more intense over the years, and as I experienced more traumatic events. I had plans A-Z and 1-10, just to be sure I could handle what came my way. Troubleshooting and analyzing for my corporate job came naturally. I could spot a potential issue a mile away.

Trauma and wounding that I remembered from my childhood, teen years, and as I was becoming a young adult. It left an indelible mark. (Or so I thought, it's getting lighter and lighter all the time, through the work.) I thought being a survivor was something I had to announce and live up to being. Over the years, I've learned so much about myself. One thing I heard during my self-care meditation is that I no longer needed to survive, and neither do others.

Are you a survivor of life? When did this survivor badge get claimed for you?

For me, I was raised a survivor. There is something I feel inside when I connect to the word survivor and what it used to mean. There is pride and strength, and ego. Raised by a single mother, I knew what surviving looked like. It was making it, no matter what. Looking back, this is so limiting. This limiting belief has shown up in so many ways.

I will never forget the day my mother sat me down in my sophomore year of high school and gave me a choice. In front of me was the OCROC, Regional Occupational Center's programs for the next school year. Become a pharmacy technician or a phlebotomist while in high school, for FREE!

> ***Serenity Maven Tip:*** *My Mom always found free. A way to qualify that we were poor, I thought. Instead of the fact that we were low income in an upper-middle-class community. There was a shame I carried, and I still feel the embarrassment in my belly as I type now. Thank you for this awareness. This will be coming up in more ways, I'm sure. I don't have to figure it out. I will just trust that my awareness will grow as it needs to. I will have new experiences and exposures that will shift my perspective, with love for myself. This is the same for you.*

Magic Johnson had recently announced he was HIV positive, which rocked the country. I swiftly said no to drawing blood, out of fear, which left becoming a pharmacy technician. During my junior and senior years of high school, as my mother was going through Chemotherapy, I was navigating the life of a wild teen expressing the pain and chaos of caring for my dying mother.

Que the superhero cape. But it was going to be OK! I had a plan to survive. I WAS A SURVIVOR! I GOT THIS!

It wasn't until two years ago, during meditations, that I realized for the past 25 years I have been surviving AS PLANNED! I WAS BEING AN AMAZING SURVIVOR.

TRIGGER WARNING BELOW:

What are some types of life experiences and traumas do survivors live through?

- Loss of a parent or loved one from Drinking & Driving
- Loss of a parent or loved one to cancer or other terminal illness
- Narcissistic Abuse
- Sexually assaulted, date raped, gang-raped
- Drug abuse
- Becoming a teen parent or having multiple children as a teen
- Domestic Violence
- Lived through an attempted murder
- Miscarriage/Loss of a child
- Parent of a child who has been on life support
- Parent of multiple children with medical journeys

TRIGGER WARNING ABOVE

What if I told you I had a survivor badge for every single one of those? And I earned them before I was the age of 21? When I tell you I knew trauma, it was non-stop. I used to say all the time, "If it's bad and it's going to happen, it's going to happen to me." THIS was my life mantra! I believed it and I lived it. And what may offend others I MANIFESTED IT AND I CREATED IT!

No, I didn't deserve the shit that happened. But I believed I did and from that space of thinking, my life continued to spiral out of control. Each step, moving further from my truth as I took action that went against my gut feelings and intuition.

I had been through things, and I had a right to be angry, bitter, frustrated. I had been through things that allowed me to focus on why I was limited, and the story behind it. and ignoring the impact of my limitations. I surrounded myself with those who believed the same. Even as I say this now, I still have an inkling of who am I upsetting my saying this. But I am sharing it for a reason.

When I heard these words at face value, I was offended and pissed off. Who would tell a survivor not to be one? When I decided my life had to change for my own happiness, I had to admit that maybe how I was doing things just wasn't working. Regardless of labels, words, or terms.

What if I just stripped it down to who I needed to BE now and focused on being that? What if I stopped making excuses with my shitty truths and used the experiences and memories to see how they were limiting me? I decided to do this. You can too.

That anxiety, stress, depression, sickness - whatever the labels you have are, how heavy of a release is it when you give yourself permission to just be love as of right now. In this very moment, and going forward, you will be aware of when things are not in alignment?

It doesn't mean you get to ignore your heavy past. It simply means you're no longer willing to carry it around and be limited to your old story. That you are the creator of your truth. You are the creator of your destiny.

Can you relate to the impact this one feeling and state of being had on me for my entire life?

Anxiety, as a word, felt like an understatement. My belly felt like a rat was always running on a wheel; it was simply a matter of how fast. At times, I was literally living in fight or flight mode.

Yet still claiming I was surviving. I had to live up to that.

Inside I was a mess. Feeling like a fraud. Falling apart inside. Until that started to turn into bitterness, anger, and eventually rage. I was being NICE. (Not Intentionally Creating Energy).

Two lives. One at work/with my friends and one at home. I was so easy to set off.

THIS CONTINUED FOR NEARLY TWO DECADES

TWO DECADES.

Did you read that? Two, too many decades! My jaw dropped. I hope yours did too! Who in their right mind would tolerate this unhappiness for so long? But excuse me If you are A-HEM! If you are reading this, dear ones, there is something you have been tolerating for far too long. But no worries, we're only almost halfway through the life-creating Guide to Balanced Wellness. I would say life-changing, but you don't need to change. You just need to allow your authentic self to be. To BE YOU TO BE LOVE and TO SHINE BRIGHT like only YOU are meant to shine!

You are learning the tools and the steps to do the work to create balance and happiness. You ARE worthy. You ARE love. Now it's time to do the work to intentionally live and define your core beliefs, and then align your mindset and actions through intentional living. Releasing the belief and behaviors tied to being N.I.C.E. and PERFECT.

One last thing about intentions. PERFECTIONISTS listen up here.

You are not alone. You are fully supported by your God of Understanding/Universe/Spirit/Source. All you have to do is set the intention and allow the synchronicities and nudges to guide you.

Say what!?!?!? Yes! I'm telling you this on space where the feeling of FREEDOM comes from. You no longer have to be perfect. I know it sounds skeptical. I was a HUGE skeptic. But just pretend with me that it will work for you as it has for me and my clients. You'll have a lifetime to test it out!

As I learned to trust, I've seen my life shift, and I've seen myself grow in awareness. As I grew in awareness of myself, I appreciate others more. I am able to expand being love. Over time I have been working through the areas with deeper trauma, even as recently as this month. I was so shocked and blindsided by the awareness and the impact on my personal healing journey, and I shared it openly and spontaneously in a podcast episode. I trust intentional living so much, and I often use intention as an alarm clock. "I need to be awake before 4:00 am".

Now, of course, we can still sabotage manifesting/creating with intentions, because we don't just send out vibrations with thoughts and words, but also our feelings. So, if you are saying and thinking one thing, but deep inside you feel differently, this will all affect your vibe and what you are sending out and attracting back to you. You have to do energy work as well. Mindset is not enough. Especially if you have doubts about the words or thoughts you have.

Every time I share about these experiments with new people, their minds are blown. It's one of those things that you can quickly apply to other areas of your life. You may be doing that now, as they have. Where they suddenly start connecting the dots to make sense of their own life experiences, realizing we are 70% water. In chapter 2, we talked about vibration and energy. As well as how the moon energy affects the ocean, the largest body of water and how it also affects us and all living things.

Now we're going to apply another layer of awareness to how much we are affected by what is happening around and through us as highly sensitive beings. Have you stopped to consider the vibrational frequency of your thoughts and words? How that affects your whole self: body, mind, and spirit.

Dear one, there is no leaving you out on this life-altering info. DNA and epigenetic altering info. I'm going to share with you now what you need to know at this moment, which is just skimming the surface. You may be drawn to explore this more. I encourage you to set the intention to be shown what you need to and be drawn to do own experiments to check the vibe in and around your spaces. You can discreetly hide the jars around your home. (Wink Wink)

In the book, Hidden Messages in Water by Dr. Masaru Emoto, he uses high-speed photography to capture what he discovered working with frozen water. "He found that water from clear springs and water that has been exposed to loving words shows brilliant, complex, and colorful snowflake patterns. In contrast, polluted water, or water exposed to negative thoughts, forms incomplete, asymmetrical patterns with dull colors." (Source - Simon & Schuster - https://www.simonandschuster.com/books/Hidden-Messages-in-Water/Masaru-Emoto/9780743289801)

It is so amazing to see! You're invited to check out some of the pictures of the frozen water experiment. You can find the link at http://bit.ly/serenitymaventoolbox

A family that learned about the book tried their own experiment. You may have seen either or both the water and rice experiments floating around on the internet. Or maybe even the version where it's a plant that is what is shown as affected by positive and negative words. This one here though didn't even have to be spoken to. Simply the energy of the label applied to it was enough to negatively affect the vibe.

This is where cutting cords in chapter 3 is important. When we aren't aware of the energetic connections, we can be affected simply by what other things or say about us. And vice versa. When you are low vibe and negative about others, they are affected and feel it too. WE ARE ALL HIGHLY SENSITIVE BEINGS. Just some of us are numb to actually being or have found another label to justify how you are showing up and being. This reminds me of another experiment where kids live up to what was expected of them. Hmmm. I'm connecting dots even further now. Are you?

> **Serenity Maven Tip:** *If you ever meet someone who knows everything and isn't willing to be open-minded. 1, 2, 3-RUN!*

So back to the rice experiment, the family cooked some regular white rice. They separated it into 3 jars. They then set the intention to label each jar with how that particular jar will be treated. The first had positive and loving words, the next had negative and hateful words, and the last was simply left alone and neglected. Despite their intentions to speak to the jars daily, they actually forgot about their experiment for about 6 months. However, the experiment continued!

The thoughts, labels, and exposures when the jars were created were enough to affect each jar uniquely. Here was the surprising outcome of that experiment.

1) The jar with positive and loving words was practically free of any bacteria
2) The jar with negative and hateful words was packed with many forms of bacteria
3) The jar that was simply left alone, neglected had some bacteria growth, but certainly nowhere close to the one that had negative and hateful words.

Salt, Vinegar, Water Activity: This one actually draws the toxic energy to clear it, but you can visibly see the energy. Add two tablespoon each of salt and vinegar to a 16-ounce glass or jar of water. Mis well and set in a place where you tend to spend a lot of time. You can do it in multiple rooms. Leave it alone for at least an entire day. Once the salt stops rising in the glass, it is done.

We also tried this for a couple of days and I will be continuing this one! It says it helps to draw out the negative energy.

Wasn't that fun?!?! Reminds me of science class, one of my favorite topics in school. Before you move along to your activities for this chapter, let's stop and set some intention!

Here's to intentionally living in the moment, creating a balanced life in alignment with your own intuitively guided core beliefs!

Xoxo

PS: If I haven't told you lately, You are doing GREAT! You are ENOUGH! You are WORTHY!!

Serenity Maven Activity #10 - Your Awareness Level

1. I had no idea what intentional living was. I was "living the dream" of getting up and repeating the same thing every day. A life I was told I had to accept. I can't change, because it would just be so different and not what is expected of me.
2. I am opening up and becoming more aware of my life being out of alignment with my life purpose. I don't yet know what my life purpose is, but I feel I am here to make a difference for the wellbeing of our planet and the lives of others.
3. I am open. I am aware of my life purpose. I am beginning to experience what flow is. It's something I realize I need more of.
4. I am in flow most of them. I am intentionally living my life, aligning with my life purpose.
5. I am in complete flow. I am intentionally living my life in alignment with my life purpose.

After reading the descriptions of 1-5 above, intentionally answer the following questions. To do this, simply close your eyes. Please one hand on your heart and one hand on your belly. Take a nice slow breath in through your nose and out through your mouth. As you connect, ask yourself the answers. Trust your truth. There is no right or wrong. This is simply an activity to align your authentic core beliefs, your mindset, and your actions. We must create the muscle memory to shift. You were raised to conform, be nice, and to do as you were told. Even when you saw and heard things you knew were not right, you were forced to create a way to survive in this environment. It is very easy to "slip back" into unconscious, unintentional actions on "auto-pilot" that you've been using to survive. The Gem opportunities of awareness are your gift and pressure points that will allow you to connect and thrive.

Although thriving BEING intentional and living in a way that you are aligning your core beliefs, mindset and actions. Some may think thriving means everything in life "goes your way." Thriving is a state of being that allows you to respond instead of reacting while connecting to your intuition, creating a lifestyle of intentions is going to take time. Through this process, you are creating balance, happiness, trust, and truth. You are BEING authentic.

Let's check in with your new awareness. Here are a couple of Serenity Maven Activities. You will be checking in - with INTENTION - by CONNECTING. Start by closing your eyes, taking a breath, allowing yourself to feel connected, and then ask yourself the questions below in this activity.

> **Serenity Maven Tip:** WHATEVER it is you hear, see, feel, or know WRITE IT DOWN, draw it if you see shapes. Again, no matter what it is, or as crazy or as far off from what you've ever thought your entire life. Don't dismiss anything.
>
> Shout out for this handed down lesson - Thank you, Monika Kali, at Fierce Love Yoga.
>
> THIS changed the entire game for me! Here is what came up that very first time I tried this in her studio. I was bitten by 3 dogs growing up, and I got to work with dogs shelters. It was the last thing I thought I would do. When I applied the rule: Don't dismiss anything, crazy stuff I would never think of came up! Today, as a Reiki Master Teacher, I teach others to help dogs, and while I have not yet worked with dogs in shelters, I can see working with dogs in shelters in my future at some point. I'm very drawn to it now. You are a

master manifester. *If you feel like your manifesting is "broken," it's not. ALL of your energy is used to create. There is more healing to do. Not that you aren't whole, but the frequency at which the energy is vibing in your body needs to rise. You know that saying "Raise Your Vibe"... it's not JUST a saying. It's been passed down for generations for a reason.*

Serenity Maven Activity #11 - Intentional Living

Allow the first number you hear, feel, see, or know. Your primary intuitive gift will be the strongest right now if you've not been tapping into using your gifts. TRUST. There are no wrong answers. This is more about trusting the process of knowing you already know.

What level of intention am I living in now?
0 1 2 3 4 5

What level(s) of intention have I been in previously?
0 1 2 3 4 5

What level of intention feels like where I want to be?
0 1 2 3 4 5

Continue checking in for each question. No skimping or rushing, dear one! You live in a rushed world. The only one who will make time for you is YOU. I PROMISE you. If you don't make time. It will not happen.

What do I need to do to live at the level I desire?

_____

_____

What do I need to do over the next year to support this desire?

_____

_____

_____

What do I need to do over the next month to support this desire?

_____

_____

_____

What do I need to do today to support this desire?

_____

_____

_____

Serenity Maven Activity #12 - Connected Free Writing

You're invited to connect to your best self and free write/journal, which is connected to your God of Understanding and the Universe. You may be starting to really understand now how I am literally breaking down the steps and taking you through the actions so that you not only understand what I am saying, but you feel and experience it for yourself, and you can get the understanding from your own personal experience.

Say this affirmation out loud. Allow yourself to feel it, believe it, see it, and/or know it. Just be. Just allow. Whatever comes up or how it comes up. Even if it comes by way of images or single words. How you connect and receive is unique to you and your unique gifts. Through experiences, you will learn to interpret your messages further. Like any muscle, your intuition and guidance will grow stronger daily. Don't use it and you will fall back to old habits and patterns.

I am intentionally living.
I am committed to living my authentic life.
I am destined to simply be me.
I am defining my authentic self.
I do this by allowing all I have been taught and exposed to from conception to be questioned.
I am allowed to define my own core beliefs and authentic truths.
As I connect with myself daily, I allow myself the time to reconnect and get to know myself.
Who I really am.
I am LOVE.
I am BALANCED.
I am FLOW.
I am GRATITUDE.
I am HAPPINESS.
I am a light meant to shine brightly. I am worthy of all the abundance the universe has to offer.
As I align my mindset and actions with my core beliefs and authenticity, I am creating my dream life.
I am creating Balanced wellness.
I am achieving Targeted Wellbeing.

What is the message from my highest and best self? What do I know I need to allow to come through? What are the whispers saying?

Great work! You are doing AWESOME!!

Dear one, it's time to trust that you know. Through this experience, you will need to be grounded and centered. Especially as you encounter people, places, and things that are no longer in alignment with the vibration you are raising to. There are all kinds of terms and words, but essentially experiences and exposures that drain you or trigger you to react versus respond. Let's dive into grounding and centering in the next chapter. But that was A LOT of work. Give yourself some time to integrate all you have learned, but don't let too much time go by.

Set your alarm now to come back to this guidebook 5-7 days from now. If you need more time then, set another alarm 5-7 days out. You can keep resetting, but don't leave yourself in the dark with old sabotaging behaviors. This is important to you. It's time to be sure your actions are aligned. Your future self will thank you.

Chapter 5

GROUNDING AND CENTERING

GROUNDING VS. CENTERING

Is there a difference? Yes, there is. Both are essential and purposeful, but they are different. You must be grounded, then centered to be aligned. This is in many senses - physically, emotionally, mentally and spiritually. As you align your vibe/essence with your truth, this is spiritual alignment. You've been learning that defining your core beliefs is done over time. It's a process, using the same steps over and over as a lifestyle, as you become spiritually aligned in your core beliefs, mindset, and actions.

Imagine a tree. It's roots keep it grounded. The trunk keeps it centered. Without the roots, the trunk cannot stand against the weather. Without the trunk, the roots have nothing to keep grounded.

You are the same. Grounding helps you to stay in place, regardless of what is going on around you. You know where you stand and are firm in your understanding. You are more responsive than reactive because you are grounded in your core beliefs. In those areas you are not as grounded, you are more reactive. You get pressured, and you move your position because you are looking to outside sources. This is where centering comes in. When you are grounded in your core beliefs, you are centered on the foundation of your authentic truths.

My thoughts racing. Just like the energy in a wire needs grounding for excess energy, so do all things. When I am not grounded, I feel like I'm going a million miles a minute. It's not so extreme now, because I use my tools when I feel ungrounded. However, before I ever intentionally grounded, I was A HOT MESS! I cannot even imagine being exposed to my energy. My adult children say am a full 180 degrees from the Mom who raised them. As hard as that is to swallow, I'm sure glad I am no longer in that space, and so are they.

My clients often say they feel anxious or all over the place. Through my own experiences, as well as my client's experiences, I have found a new way to manage these feelings. When the feelings start, start with step 1. Decide you ready to manage your vibe and then go into the steps you have been learning.

1. Decide you want what is in alignment with your highest good and the highest good of all.
2. Create A Peaceful Space
3. Connect to your best self and your God of Understanding/Universe/Spirit/Source
4. Set your Intention
5. Center and Ground
6. Live in the moment
7. Release the past
8. Envision the future
9. Trust Yourself
10. Rinse and repeat

You may have heard these steps before and wondered why closing your eyes and asking/praying to release the past, trust, and live in the moment as you move forward wasn't working. You may have even wondered if your ability to manifest was "broken." It's not that at all. You will have to look at what you've been avoiding.

You don't have to go back to relive your traumatic experiences. But you do have to be willing to look at how the emotions from experiences are influencing how you are showing up, or not showing up for yourself and others today. You do have to be willing to allow love, with an open heart and mind. Extend to yourself the compassion you have been screaming for.

There is a saying that no one can do for you what you are not willing to do for yourself. Do you hear that? You have to be willing to care for yourself the way you want to be cared for. And if you're really honest, do you hold back in fear of being hurt - yet wonder why others are holding back from you?

Imagine being fully authentic. Fully visible. Fully heard. Supported by a like-minded tribe, with the same mission to be authentic, be love, be loved, and shine brighter. If this calls to your heart and soul, you are part of the new era. The new way of loving. The new way of being. It's no longer time to focus on trying to change those who are not ready or willing to be love. It's time to be self-centered. To raise your own vibration, to uniquely shine your light on the world. As you do, those who are meant to be together will be.

One reason many of us on this planet have been living uncentered is you have been raised to believe that being self-centered is selfish. It is furthest from selfish. It is ESSENTIAL. By not taking care of yourself first, you are simply depleted and drained of your own energy.

To really understand what we are talking about, let's apply some simple things that most of us can agree on, as proven through science and physics.

1) Everything has energy
2) The sun and the moon affect the ocean/tides
3) You are more than 70% of water
4) Just as the ocean's flow is affected by the sun and moon, your energy/vibe/flow is affected.

Serenity Maven Tip You can do some google searches on this one and try using the sun and moon energy yourself to see how you are affected. Decide based on your own experiences.

Now let's walk through some personal experiences you have all the time when you think about it.

1) You can sense when someone's "vibe is off"
2) When you are around upbeat people, you are upbeat
3) There are certain people who drain you. Just from being around them.
4) You've felt the life sucked out of the room before
5) Have you ever heard of how chaotic and crazy the full moon night is first responders or emergency rooms?

These were some things I was aware of, but not at the level of awareness where I was doing something about it. Heck, I didn't even know you could do something about it. Grounding was the first tool that really helped me with staying calm. Being able to then look for my center and realize if my center was off. We'll get to centering in just a moment but let's start with grounding

Grounding is a way to protect your energy. It is one of those things that is essential. Ground every morning. If you also have a nightly routine, grounding at night will also help you. There are times where experiences and exposures are so low vibe, that you may have to ground repeatedly in order to navigate from a space where you can remain looking at the experience from a space of love.

There are a couple of ways to ground in guided meditations, and in meditation time, you can set the intention to ground and visually take yourself through the process of grounding. I usually like to start in the heart space and envision some sort of connector down to the Center of the Earth. There are other times where you need to ground much quicker, and you won't have the time to do that. This is where intention comes in. Intention is everything. There is no need to be the perfectionist. Right? So, there are times where just saying the word "ground" or thinking the word "ground" is enough.

Being able to just say the word ground or think the word ground is going to help you when you are around what is commonly known as an energy vampire an energy vampire is someone who is not responsible with their own energy and when they come around their energy is very large and wide and consuming to other people and still as a highly sensitive person you are aware of these folks.

You probably have people in your own family, in your current circles, or maybe even people you workaround that may drain you. Here is a simple technique. The last time I shared about this I was joking that it is "The Grounding Song", because at times I've had to say it repeatedly around certain people. But seriously, it is literally what I do in my own mind and you can do this yourself if you can just say the word ground.

Serenity Maven Tip: *There are times where you just feel like you keep getting ungrounded around certain people. You ground and continue to get knocked off your pedestal of being solid and grounded. Use "The Ground Song" to help you combat becoming ungrounded. Simply, while they're talking, just say repeatedly over and over and over the words, "ground ground ground ground ground ground ground." For fun, I like to make it a son. You can even do it to the tune of a song. You can choose to have a little fun with it. That try it out and see how that helps you the next time you are around that person that just repeatedly makes you feel "off". This tool is one that my clients tend to thank me for. It is also one that I use less as I build stronger and firmer boundaries with the people in my life who I labeled as energy vampires. To support this, I have been able to extend compassion and forgiveness, and we'll talk about that in Chapter 7 - Release the Past.*

As the past has been released, I have been able to create firm boundaries and those people are not my life. Unless they're going to respect me and respect my space, they are not welcome. The boundaries you create will support you as you continue to move forward, taking steps in alignment with your true authentic core beliefs. You will continue to shape your life into a space with peace, love, happiness, and success. Those are really what you are at your truth. As you are becoming more and more aligned, you are attracting others who are aligned as well.

> ***Serenity Maven Tip:*** *It's important to know that as a highly sensitive person, you may in fact be an energy vampire to others. So while this is a hard pill to swallow it is important to note that if you have not been aware and mindful and using tools to manage your own energy, you may be using your own energy to (for lack of better term) "dump" on others in situations where you may have been triggered. Unintentionally sharing your*

energy. All this might suck to hear this it is important to be aware of this so that you can connect deeper with those around you who are wanting to connect with you.

CENTERING

As we already talked about centering is more about the trunk of the tree versus the roots. You can think of centering as being balanced. When you're off balance, you are off-center. In order to re-center, you have to take action. This is why I call it being self-centered. You may have always been told that being self-centered was wrong, or it was selfish. **Being self-centered is, in fact, essential.**

One more time for the really stubborn ones. Ahem. You. Right here in the front

BECOMING CENTERED INVOLVES BEING SELF-CENTERED.

Not only do you have permission to be self-centered, you now have a responsibility. A responsibility to be aware of your own energy and your own sense of being centered and grounded. All this responsibility might sound daunting. this is all just new to you at a conscious level or a reminder at a conscious level at a subconscious level. This is familiar territory. Something that you've already signed up for, so take a deep breath. Let's look at the awesome things about this responsibility. The awesome thing about this responsibility is there is a gift that comes with it. This gift is the ability to be in the moment. When you find yourself not being in the moment check-in with yourself. Are you centered? Are you grounded? Do you need to go through all the steps to connect? If so, connect, feel it, pray and ask for the Miracles to release and support being centered and balanced.

Centering and grounding are the key gifts that you will receive when you do yourself care. Every single day this is what is part of filling your cup first. You fill your cup first so that you can serve from your saucer. (Thank you to Lisa Nichols for this gem!) When you say you're too busy and your life is too crazy and chaotic to give yourself the time, this is the time to balance, center, ground clear, and activate. If not, you are setting yourself up for failure in your day. It's no different than if you see your gas tank on empty and you try to drive all the way to your destination. You're no different. In fact, you are even more regulated than the computers are in your vehicle. Your body is miraculous, but it is not limitless. Your physical body has limits, and it is essential that you take care of it

As someone who is here to serve the world, to shine your light, it is even more essential and critical that you are serving yourself first. If you continue to go out and serve others without serving yourself first, you will show up sicker and sicker and sicker. Whether it be because you're resentful, angry and bitter these emotions can show up as physical sickness from the dis-ease, or lack of ease, showing up as disease.

You're now halfway through this Guide to Balanced Wellness. Well done, by the way! You know that self-care and taking care of yourself is more than just shopping or getting your nails done. Although that can be added from time to time. When it comes to really giving yourself the self-care and connection you need, you may be giving it 100%, but if not, don't stress. You have given it more than ZERO effort, which says a lot! You're invited now to commit even more to your purpose of living a lifestyle of balance and ease and flow. (Pssst pssst reminder - the more that you have to enjoy, the more that you can share with others, and the more you can serve.)

Ready? Committed to more for yourself and the life you desire to create and live? There is action behind the belief, desire, and dream. Now is the time to take the action.

Go into your alarm and set it now for every single morning. Get up at least 20 minutes earlier than you do to give yourself the time for your daily self-care routine if you are seeking a deeper healing. Journey you're invited to set that alarm 60 minutes, up to two hours before your usual time. If you do the math 20 minutes of self-care of deep meditation is equivalent to one hour of rested sleep. Making one hour of meditation the equivalent of 4 hours of restful sleep. Guess what that means? If you are tired, you can make up that time that you lost by getting up 2 hours earlier. You don't even have to physically get out of bed. You can simply get up, put on some music or a guided meditation. You can do this before getting out of bed. As you move forward in the coming weeks, and in the coming months, you can expand your goal to get up and out and sit and get all of the fun stuff out with the candles in the crystals and the sage to amplify your self-care time.

The most important thing to do here, while gently stepping out of your comfort zone, is to commit to only what you will really do. Start with 5 minutes and work your way up to 20 minutes if you have to. I started in my sleep and then worked up to 2-hour sessions, while deep healing in the beginning. 20 minutes is considered daily maintenance.

Let's ground and center now.

Serenity Maven Activity #12 - Ground and Center

Dear one you are invited now to set the intention to receive and allow. Be mindful of being grounded, centered. As well as grateful and filled with love for all the Miracles around. You're invited to take a moment to stop and put one hand on your heart one hand on your lower belly to connect. Breathe in through your nose and out through your mouth showing gratitude. Envisioning grounding taking place from your heart space down to the center of the earth. Envisioning centering.

If you feel off-centered, what is it that's pulling you? What is that pressure? What is that saying to you to connect with it? Acknowledge it, feel it, and ask it anything you need to. Acknowledge your guides and your team of angels. Ask and pray for the support that you need. Allowing this to re-center and ground you; bringing you a sense of calmness and a sense of peace and hope and happiness as you feel like you are in the space you need to be spiritually, mentally and spiritually.

Here are some questions to ask yourself while grounded and centered:

1) What does it feel like in my body?
2) What does it sound like in my mind?
3) What does it feel like in my vibe/spirit?
4) What does it feel like emotionally?
5) What specific emotions do I feel?

Honor all your feelings, dear one. No matter if they are a high vibe or low vibe. Denying your true emotions, thoughts, and feelings have led you to where you were. Your authentic, loving voice is allowed to be heard. When you feel heard, it's easier to shift into living in the moment. Let the words and emotions up and out. Be in this moment; present, grounded and centered.

Well done! Take a deep breath. Let's talk about what it looks like to LIVE in the moment, beyond just BEING in the moment. I'll see you in chapter 6 soon! Xoxo Mama Honey

> ***Serenity Maven Tip:*** *Using the Moon energy for meditation is one of my favorite ways to harness the moon energy. It can be used to manifest Miracles, healing, clearing, and receiving. You're invited to join us online for LIVE events or to access recordings of the guided meditations.*

To access the online LIVE events or recordings go to: http://bit.ly/serenitymaventoolbox

Chapter 6

BEING IN THE MOMENT

Live in the moment! This may sound so cliché. But what does living in the moment actually look like? When you think of this phrase, "Live in the moment," what do you envision?

For me, I wanted to be able to slow down, think, and talk slower and I wanted to be able to joyfully laugh from my gut. Like REALLY laugh. Although I'm known for my smile and laughing, it wasn't a "full" laugh, if you know what I mean. More than a giggle and not fully ENJOYED while doing it.

I remember the first time I spoke to my healing teacher Sarah Christine Nolan. She was calm. She was Zen. She was everything I wasn't. I was a HOT MESS and past my boiling point I had boiled over and fizzled out. When I think back now to what that felt like, I'm going to just stop right here and now with gratitude and celebration. Do you have anything in this very moment to be grateful for? Close your eyes, breathe, and fill with gratitude. What are you grateful for right now? What are you doing right at this very moment that you are grateful for?

Perhaps

- Your breath
- The senses that you have the ability to use: Sight, Hearing, Touching, Feeling, Tasting. (If you are limited in any of these, focus on your abilities).
- Your heartbeat and all that is because of it
- Your present awareness
- You are alive, which in itself is enough to create opportunities
- Having hope. Realizing that things can shift for you and they are.
- Add any of your own as many as you can think of. No wasting time when it comes to gratitude.

_____

_____

_____

_____

_____

Let's check in about being present. When you are doing an activity or at an event, are you enjoying what is happening at the event, or are you busy with your smartphone taking pictures and videos to capture the moment for the future. Have you ever thought of where your focus is when you are doing that? Are you thinking about the future? Focused on capturing the moments, but not fully engaged at the moment, what are you missing out on? Are you focused on capturing the perfect moment to post on social media?

In the words of Lady J, "You don't need that! Leave your phone here. Let's go to the park!" Are you engaged in your own actual life? In today's fast-paced world, the demands can be overwhelming and overbearing. For those with professional careers, families, homes, and other obligations, there is actually an official diagnosis for burn-out from the WHO/ World Health Organization.

BURNOUT DEFINED

Per the WHO's website, Bur-out is a syndrome conceptualized as resulting from chronic workplace stress that has not been successfully managed. It is characterized by three dimensions:

- feelings of energy depletion or exhaustion; increased mental distance from one's job,
- or feelings of negativism or cynicism related to one's job; and
- reduced professional efficacy.

Source: https://www.who.int/mental_health/evidence/burn-out/en/

As I am working on this chapter, I am reading Day 5 of *Marianne Willaimson's, **A Year of Miracles - Daily Devotions and Reflections**. I struggled with writing this guidebook from the pressure of my own ego. And now, in my own gem opportunity of awareness, I acknowledge the shame and guilt. Connected, grounded, and centered, I can feel it, even more. I pray and ask to release any fears. And now the divinely timed message I read today on Day 5 all makes sense. I will share my vulnerabilities and the synchronicities in my own life. This doesn't mean I am excused for missing the deadline. This means when I veer off track/off task, I am still guided, protected and loved. Just as you are.

So just like you, I had to surrender, surrender to my truth surrender to my purpose in this very moment I'm closing my own eyes I'm breathing in and connecting. In this space, I ask and pray for Miracles of healing and knowing. How do I know when I am healed?

You know what living in the past and living the future feels like. Healed is living in the present moment. But what does living in the moment consist of? Living in the moment is a way of being. To be aware of what is happening around you and through you. To choose to make decisions in alignment with your core beliefs and aligned mindset. To surrender. To trust that you are divinely guided, protected, and safe. To believe in the synchronicities and live in gratitude when you see them.

Doesn't this sound amazing? Where does one even start when they have a lifetime of choices made out of obligations and fears? How does it happen?

The answer is very simple.

You start right now. At this very moment, you can set the intention. You can choose to align with your destiny by living and being authentic in every moment. You can choose to surrender to trust.

You can use your authentic voice, which is loving. You choose to say yes to what feels right to you. You choose to say no to what doesn't feel right for you.

You choose to simply be you. Which is love? YOU ARE LOVE! It may feel like such a contrast to how you have been reacting. But at this moment, you can choose to show up as love. To see yourself, others, and the world through a lens of love.

Layer by layer, the experiences and exposures from your past will come to your awareness when you are ready to heal. Are you ready?

Let's try it now.

Imagine a time you felt soooo much in love. Feel that feeling. Capture it, remember it. Pretend you can now direct that love towards yourself. As you fill up with this feeling of love (aka Raise Your Vibe)

You may be feeling married to being angry and bitter or upset. You may even realize you like that story. Not that you enjoy it. But that it is so familiar that you subconsciously align your reactions, your emotional responses to what is familiar.

What about the opposite. What about a time you didn't capture the moments and had regrets over it. Are those keeping you from living in the moment?

It's important to look at your blocks. Without looking at the blocks, it will be difficult to live in the moment and to manifest in alignment with your highest good. We'll explore releasing the past in the next chapter, but for now, let's dive more into living in the moment.

Recognizing when you're not living in the moment is important. I would share with you how to recognize when you're living in the moment, but when you're living in the moment, you are doing just that, and you won't be thinking about living in the moment. When you are lost in thinking about stress, worries, and thinking about all of the negative possibilities you are so focused on the future (or the past) that you don't even have an awareness of your own physicality (your own body, the things around you, the space you fill). Take a moment now to start looking out around you completely. Looking around in the space you are in. Looking down, looking at your hands, looking at your feet and recognizing that you are present and aware and fully living in this moment.

On my healing journey I have awakened to new levels of awareness repeatedly. I will continue to do this for my lifetime, just as you will. But before I started on my journey, I was stuck in the past. I was stuck in regrets. I was stuck from not being connected with who I truly am. I would walk across the parking lot to pay for gas at the gas station, and I would look at the ground. I would put my makeup on and I would look at the makeup being put on my eye, but I wouldn't actually connect with myself and look at myself in my own eyes. I was not connected with being in the present moment. I was unaware. Unaware of my own energy, presence and how my vibe was affecting others. At the same time, I was fully aware of how the energy of others was affecting me.

> ***Serenity Maven Tip*** - *A couple of years into my journey now I have healed so many things, yet there are so many other things that I still find myself reacting to the difference is now I have an awareness that I am reacting instead of responding. And this happens much sooner. I'm able to take myself through the process in a matter of minutes, hours or days, as opposed to weeks, months, years or even decades. I'm quite certain there's still plenty of things that I'm not even aware of. In time they'll come up through gem opportunities awareness. Being gentle and being curious when that happens is something that I taught myself. I share that with you as something that I will continue to use the rest of my life.*

Can you relate to this? Do you go back and forth between trying to reach out and connect, but only to retreat?

We'll also talk more about forgiveness. Self-forgiveness and forgiveness of others coming up in the next chapter of releasing the past. It is important to know that forgiveness is required in order to live in the moment. If you find yourself saying you have forgiven, but your actions and words say otherwise (to be very clear) you are not living in the moment. It's time to be aware of that and work through it. You're invited to take a quick moment now, if you're ready, to ask of your God of Understanding/Universe/Spirit/Source something very simple:

"Please help me release _____. I asked for Miracles and blessings and to be filled with love to raise my vibration and the vibration of the planet. Lead me and guide me as I surrender and trust. I choose to live in the moment. Thank you."

Sometimes it can be confusing. When you have emotions from the past come up in similar experiences to the past. What we may feel is repeated experiences showing up over and over is absolutely correct. The difference will be whether you choose to react or respond, and how long it takes to respond. Or perhaps you won't even notice it because your boundaries are authentically keeping you from the exposure.

It's not just the past that can keep you from living in the now, or in the present moment. Envisioning your future is essential to set up your subconscious mind to take the actions and steps necessary to create that big vision. As a visionary, your vision is growing larger and larger and sometimes as you get closer to that vision it becomes clear. Which makes if become even bigger. It made me feel as though you're not actually getting closer to your destiny. You also have to be cautious of when you are in the space of comparing your now to the future. Getting stuck. Of course, you have to stop and look at it. However, if you're not taking action to get closer and you're just constantly looking at that future. Thinking it's going to just happen without doing the work to define your core beliefs, your authentic voice, and your mindset is a recipe for insanity. You must take the actions and to use your authentic voice to be present and in the moment.

Chapter 7

RELEASE THE PAST

Releasing the past is not a one-time thing. These 10 steps are all part of the cycles and phases of creating a LIFESTYLE of balanced wellness.

Think of those who use balance as a skill. Tight rope walkers, weighing anything from food to a baby, taking an adventure outdoors, and simply walking. Balance is something that takes care and awareness, conscious, and or subconscious. Balances are applied when something can go in either direction. A lot versus nothing. Left versus Right. Towards your destiny versus away from your destiny.

That is what is needed from you, dear one. You need to focus on creating the balance you desire. You must create the changes to align with your destiny in this lifetime, or you will regret it. You don't have to do it; the choice is yours. I guarantee you will be happier if you do. You will continue to have regrets from guilt and shame if you do not.

To move towards your destiny, aligning your core beliefs, mindset, and actions - including speaking with your authentic voice is essential. This will require you to first define your core beliefs. This will also require you to define your target for your wellbeing, to support envisioning your future. This is more than just sitting down and writing a list. It is a process. The whole process is laid out herein, **The Serenity Maven's Guide to Balanced Wellness**, with the cycle, phases, and steps.

With over 1 million things per second that your mind processes and being what important will come to the front of your awareness, you will continue to have these "Gem opportunities of awareness." These are moments where you will become aware of something no longer in alignment with who you want to be, as your authentic and best version of yourself. In these moments, being open is essential. An open mind and an open heart. Remaining gentle and curious.

Referencing back to the phases of healing, releasing current life patterns and family patterns is Phase 3. The more open and grateful you are, the more Miracles you are willing to receive. Achieving popcorn speed is amazingly awe dropping. (You're invited to try it!)

Releasing current life patterns will require you to do some work. In addition to the daily self-care time, time to work through healing is essential as well. I recommend to my clients 1-2 hours of deep connection every day, just as I did over about 6 months' time, to allow for the time necessary.

The development of your essence/vibe started from the time of conception through experiences and exposures. We'll now go through learning about your energy channels. It didn't make sense to me until it did. If you're not familiar with the terminology of chakras, I'm going to ask you to be open. If you do know about chakras, get ready to deepen that understanding so you can use it to propel you forward on your journey. This information here is my message to the world and drives my mission. Did I just bring you through this to teach you about chakras? Hmmmmm. Perhaps I did? But keep trusting yourself on this journey. Check-in. Does this feel right? Follow your steps 1. Decide, 2. Create A Peaceful Space, 3. Connect, 4. Intention, 5. Centered, 6. Focused, & Grounded 7. Living in the moment, 8. Release the past - acknowledge the feelings, ask for Miracles.

First, when it comes to your energy channels, whether you believe in them or not, they exist. Anything I teach or share, I openly welcome you to challenge the information just as my skeptical mind did. For over 6 months. Even when I consistently saw the results, including saving my own life multiple times during a health crisis, that had me at the brink of death. CHALLENGE AWAY, dear one!! You may just be as surprised as I have been and still am.

Let's think about it. There are developmental charts for physical grown, and emotions. Did you know there are charts for your vibe too? Yes! There are! I've included a chakra development chart. And they are aligned with Erickson's Psychosocial Development chart. (That just blew my mind right there!)

What if healing your inner child was simply taking the steps outlined in this guidebook and applying a layer of knowledge about your chakras, their development, and how to activate, clear and balance your chakras? What if instead of blaming your childhood, you were able to validate all the unspoken feelings in your body and change how you are showing up in the world today? What if you had an explanation that you could then take action on by checking in and hearing your authentic voice and your true core beliefs?

Would it be possible for this secret decoder ring had the answers to a lot of your questions? Just think what if?

Are you feeling a bit like the wandering wonderer, dear one? Wonder no more. You are now wandering or re-wandering, into the world of understanding your essence and vibe even more AND more importantly, WHY following the steps in the guide will not only help you but allow you to create and live the lifestyle of balances wellness you desire.

Your ability to manifest is not broken. You are not broken. You are whole, and you are worthy of attracting all you are destined to receive. Identifying and clearing those blocks by embodying a lifestyle of balanced wellness will raise your vibration to manifest in alignment with your highest good and the highest good of all.

Are you excited and ready?!?!? Yes?! Awesome!! Let's start with what the 7 Chakras are and a little about each. We can go into hours talking about this, but this is just meant as an introduction. I really want you to experience the relief and understanding of myself and others that I felt learning this, as well as every single one of my clients.

Take a look at the Chakra Development Chart and see if there is any significance. To further support your awareness on this journey, I have a gifted offering of an 8 Day Chakra Challenge that will help you dive deep into each one on your healing journey.

Here is where you can access the 8 Day Chakra Challenge: http://bit.ly/serenitymaventoolbox

HONEY-MARIE LOVE, RMT, MLC

CHAKRA DEVELOPMENT CHART -
From Conception Throughout Life.

Life Area	Age	Chakra	Location	Color	Affected By	Affects	Affects
Survival	Conception thru 18 months	Root	Base of spine	Red	Touch	Trust & Safety Financial Health Family Health Self-Health	Birth & Reproductive Organs
Relationship	6-18 months	Sacral	Lower Belly/Lower back	Orange	Separation Experiences	Emotions & Creativity Relationship with Self, Relationship Outside Self	Ovaries & Spleen
Self-esteem	18 month - 3 years	Solar Plexus	Upper Belly/ Middle Back	Yellow	Discipline Shame Potty Training	Confidence & Decisions Performance for Self Performance for others	Adrenals, Pancreas, Stomach
Transformation	4-7 years	Heart	Chest/ Upper Back	Green	Empathy	Renewal Conscious Learning	Thymus, Heart, Circulation
Targeted Wellbeing	7-12 years	Throat	Neck up to sinus area	Blue	Criticism	Culture	Thyroid, Lungs, Ears, Nose, Throat
Make a Difference	Adolescence	Brow	Forehead	Indigo	Life Experiences	Authentic Identity Partnerships Cooperation Collaboration	Eyes, Pituitary Gland, Intuition
Service	Young Adult +	Crown	Top of head	Violet	Cutting Cords with Parents	Consciousness Social Responsibility Community	Pineal Gland, Pituitary Gland

How is this showing up in your present life?

_____

_____

Is the awareness of chakras at this level opening up a new perspective that may allow for further healing?

_____

_____

How are your loved ones affected by their own development? (parents, biological mother/father if different, grandparents, caregivers, or even your own children - born and unborn, etc. Give yourself the time to name those who come up for you. Think about each person, one by one. Think about their own inner child. Send love and show gratitude for this awareness.

_____

_____

Remaining open is important now. You may even feel as you are exposed to more information as if you already have this wisdom within you, and it is somehow being awakened. We're not diving into past lives in this guidebook, but along your journey, you will be guided to those who will help you with Phase 4 - Healing Past Life Patterns.

Releasing the past will include present and past life patterns. Some of your present life patterns, exposures and experiences from conception to now, including how you were parented, as well as epigenetics, familial dreaming patterns, and more. Releasing past life patterns and family dreaming patterns is a whole new realm of discovery for me and as I am working with my own teachers and mentors.

> **Serenity Maven Tip:** *Popcorn Speed - When you set the intention to be aware and show gratitude in moments of awareness, these moments will become more frequent. At times it will be so*

fast; when this happens, I call it Popcorn Speed. Synchronicities and Miracles popping up moment after moment, like popcorn cooking.

Dear one, now let's talk through what gem opportunities of awareness may look like

Example 1:

You are sitting at the airport, and suddenly, you find yourself engaged in the conversation. You are listening and holding space for someone. They are sharing some intimate details about themselves, and you immediately have words of wisdom for them. As you are sharing these words of wisdom, you have an awareness, a gem opportunity of awareness, for yourself. Perhaps you even have a memory that you haven't thought up for a very long time come to mind, and its memory is very similar to the one that the perfect stranger is sharing with you.

Example 2:

You are driving down the street you have the radio on, and there is either an interview or a song playing that reminds you of something from your past could be a person or an experience it could be positive it could be something that you enjoy remembering you could also be something that reminds you of a shitty truth.

It's important not to confuse high vibes and positive healing with avoiding the work and feeling the real feelings you have. It is important to recognize that looking at life through a lens of love and seeing the shitty truths is the way to heal. You have to look at it, and love doesn't necessarily mean that everything is rainbows and sunshine. Love means that you can apply compassion and see things from A New Perspective, with an open heart and an open mind.

The Finding Mommy's Soft Voice podcast is a safe space to open your heart and mind to new awareness. SOFT stands for Spiritually Open For Teaching. Without being open, nothing can be received. It's important that you are aware of when you are open and closed. And again, most importantly, gentle and curious.

> **Serenity Maven Note** - This meaning of SOFT was as shared on a live KC Miller of SWIHA, Southwest Institute of Healing Arts when she was doing a toe reading on one of my teachers and mentors, Richard Seaman. I had already intuitively named my podcast, but this new awareness brought new meaning and confirmed the name.

Often when this happens, the time you are reminded of can lead to some shame or guilt or traumatic memories. What's important is to not necessarily go into what happened and relive everything but it is important to acknowledge the feelings that are still inside you sit with them, recognize them, acknowledge them, allow yourself to feel them, feel the shitty truth, and when you acknowledge them, and reconnect with them. You can then allow yourself to ask for support to pray and ask your spirit team and guides to help heal you, to help release the blocked emotions that are showing up in your life. Blocked emotions can be showing up through sickness, through worry, through stress, through isolation to self-sabotage, through old behaviors, and habits. At this moment you may be reminded of something that is ready to be released.

You are sitting at the airport, and suddenly you find yourself sitting in the airport, and the person next to you end up engaging in a conversation, and before you know it they are sharing some intimate information about themselves and you are giving this person guidance. As you are speaking, you become aware that what you were telling this person is something that you yourself needed to hear. This is a moment where you can use this as a way to identify what needs to be released, and this would be in current life patterns and family patterns.

These are just a few. You can bring yourself through intentional awareness, just as there are opportunities throughout this guidebook and by participating in the 8 Day Chakra Challenge.

Chapter 8

ENVISIONING THE FUTURE

Vision means to see. Are you someone who sees? Daydreaming or dreaming in your sleep. Do you consider yourself a visionary? Or perhaps, someone with the gift of psychic knowing or visions? If you said yes to any of these, you have a vision. You are an amazing human being. The vessel you call your body is here to adjust to all of your needs. You have a mind that is more powerful than most realize.

Not only are you constantly changing the chemicals released to support you, you can use your thoughts and imagination, also known as visualization, to change the mind. What is real or imagined is real to the mind. Have you ever thought you lost your keys or your wallet? Even just for a moment. Your amazing body will signal a flurry of emotions and corresponding chemicals are released. Your body is now acting as if you lost your keys from the mere thought that you lost your key. They may be lost, or they could, in fact, be right where you left them, right next to you. But the thought alone could be enough to send your body through all the emotions of grief. Shock/disbelief (denial), anger, depression, bargaining, acceptance. Well, perhaps not all. Acceptance may take some time. But you get my point.

Source:
Article: Real and Imagined Movements Are Controlled by the Brain in the Same Way - Neuroscience News
https://neurosciencenews.com/real-imagined-movement-8868/

In April 2018, Neuroscience new published an article, Real and Imagined Movements Are Controlled by the Brain the Same Way. In this article, a study from the Karolinska Institute was shared. Here is the summary of that research:

Research Summary: Researchers report imagined movements can alter our sense of perception in the same ways as real movements do. The study reveals our brains predict how we would feel sensations if the imagined movements were executed.

Source: Karolinska Institute.

Now, look at that statement again, what is real or imagined, is real to the mind and allow yourself to look at all angles. What if you intentionally imagine? Can you use that to your benefit?

The answer is yes. With guided imagery, more commonly known as hypnotherapy. Many alternative/complementary therapies are clinically proven to be effective in treating trauma, including childhood trauma. Guided Imagery/Hypnotherapy is just one. Including when this shows up as a physical illness or disease. Even more amazing is that the subconscious mind can be reprogrammed, also affected the conscious mind.

"Studies have shown that practicing guided imagery may be able to: temporarily increase numbers of immune system cells to keep the rest of your body healthy, help reduce feelings of depression, increase feelings of well-being" https://www.breastcancer.org/

treatment/comp_med/types/imagery Guided Imagery article on breast cancer.org

If you're one to research, clinicaltrials.gov is a great space to look for supporting studies on guided imagery. While you're there, search these terms separately. Before you do stop, say a prayer and ask to be guided to what it is you need to know:

- Guided imagery
- Hypnotherapy
- Healing Touch
- Reiki
- Energy Healing

> **Serenity Maven Note:** *Childhood trauma vs. Trauma as an adult. While some children do experience horrific trauma or intentional/unintentional trauma through neglect, others may have experience and exposures that may not otherwise be 'deemed" as trauma by someone else. This does not minimize the experience. The emotions behind the experience are really what is important to the person experiencing it.*
>
> *As a child, the trauma is relative to the age you experienced it. One adult with abusive and traumatic life-altering experiences may be holding back on taking authentic action today just as much as an adult who was affected by expected life-altering experiences a child. Life events such as moving to a new home or the passing of a loved one, such as a grandparent can be the biggest trauma in their life. Someone who was physically abused and tortured may not see these "standard life events" instead of traumatic or life altering*

> events. The trauma that occurred doesn't matter. The emotions that were evoked can continue to be evoked/triggered. They may even become more intense in experience over time and may or may not be relative only to the actual experience that is happening in the present, but also the past. This can be referred to as repeating the underlying story.

Imagine the same emotions but showing up bigger and on different stages with different actors. There may be a different look, but the feel is very familiar. The emotional experience may be more powerful to the traumatized person with a traumatic past, than those observing from the outside. It is important that you and others feel heard. This simple form of validation and compassion can be priceless. Many life coaching clients find that to be one of the biggest benefits of their private sessions. Especially those who are highly sensitive and were told they were too sensitive, too loud, too whatever.

Can you relate, or are you just overreacting?

> **Serenity Maven Tip:** *Overreacting? Triggered? Sorry, I didn't mean to. But if you were, there something to sit with, journal on, and pray for Miracles to heal. I hear you and your feelings are REAL! The question is: Can some awareness and perspective help you shift? Ask to be shown what you need to know to move forward.*

Now that you have some new information, awareness and have done some fact checks, it's time to do some intuitive checking. Check-in now. (Yup! You've got it! Steps 1 - 7)

1. Decide
2. Create A Peaceful Space

3. Connect
4. Intention
5. Centered, Focused, & Grounded
6. Living in the moment
7. Release the past - acknowledge the feelings, ask for Miracles

As you are aware, always check-in and see what your next steps are if any. Allow yourself to dream and define your future while connected. You can write down what comes up. There are several ways to put action behind what comes up.

- Visualization
    - Use your meditation time to visualize what you desire for your future - KEEP IT BIG, DETAILED and EVOLVING
    - Guided Imagery - use specific sessions to support your future

- Vision Boards
    - Create a vision board. Electronic or tangible.
    - I like a good old-fashioned session with some magazines, scissors, glue, markers, and a big sheet of poster board.
    - Another viable option is using a software one. I like Canva.com. Super easy, and it can be saved as your screensaver on all your devices and printed out!

Serenity Maven Tip - ALLOWING - *The first time I created a meditative and intuitive vision board was at FLY, Fierce Love Yoga, with my yoga teacher Monika Kali. She passed down wisdom taught to her, to allow anything to come up. To not let anything be dismissed. I allowed sounds, words, shapes, colors, physical feelings, images, lights/start bursts, feelings, thoughts, knowing to come up, and out onto paper. This is wisdom I have shared many times and in my own vision board workshops. Allowing is essential for creating a life of balanced wellness.*

Serenity Maven Activity #14 - Envision Your Future and Best Self

This activity may be one of the most important in this Guide to Balanced Wellness. Please be sure to complete it. This guided imagery session will set up your subconscious mind to continue to move forward to create and live a lifestyle of balanced wellness.

To get your access now to the guided imagery session to envision your future and best self go-to http://bit.ly/serenitymaventoolbox

Chapter 9

TRUST YOURSELF – HEART TO HEART

Dear one, take a moment to take a relaxing breath. A nice deep breath in through your nose and out through your mouth. Let it out nice and slow. Take a moment to soak up where you are now and how far you've come from when you started this guidebook and the journey. Think about where you were in your life go back now to do the first couple of chapters and read what you have written. You have done the work to shift your awareness. To learn the steps of living an intuitive life of balanced wellness where you are checking in by connecting to your best self and source: Your God of Understanding/Universe/Spirit/Source. Grounding, Centering, and living in the moment. By doing this, you have to trust that you are guided and intuitive. Take a moment now to appreciate yourself and to show gratitude to yourself. To be thankful to yourself for showing up and for choosing to show up. Regardless of the length of time it took you to get through this guidebook, everything was divinely timed and arranged. There's no need to carry forward any judgment. You stopped making excuses and you allowed yourself the time you needed the process, adjust your mindset, and put into action the new awareness.

Dear one, you are simply enough. You now know what it is like to trust yourself as you move forward. You know to connect to your heart and intuitive wisdom and to listen to the loving voice. You can bravely trust yourself. Trust that you are no longer who you were in the past when you made decisions that went against your own intuition and knowing. You are now in a space of trusting yourself, and by trusting yourself, you are trusting that you are supported by a source greater than you - your god of understanding the universe and your spirit guide and team of angels - whatever you are comfortable with. You're trusting that you will be aware of what you need to be aware of, including those moments when you have not listened to and have taken action that is not an alignment with who you are choosing to be now.

You now have a better understanding, and you have an awareness you did not have before reading this guidebook. It will take time for when you envisioned life to become a reality. As you live in the moment and create your future in alignment with your authentic core beliefs, you are thriving! You are allowing. As you trust the flow of the universe that you have been so sensitive to, you harness the moon energy to support you even further trusting.

Your life may feel far from where you want it to be, even if this journey has been intentional for years or even decades up to this point. As you think of that, if there is any shame or guilt, allow that to come up. Use this guide to take you through it.

Literally, I just had a moment in between the last paragraph and this one. One I have not had for a while. My own shame and guilt of how is just REACTED, instead of RESPONDING with love, in alignment with my authentic core beliefs.

My belly burns. I feel frustration, anger, and rage. Emotions I was ashamed to admit before. I stuffed those emotions, and it turned into sickness and pain. Pain that has not been felt for a while. My lower back throbs. I close my eyes. Put one hand on my heart. One hand on my belly. I take a nice cleansing breath, and I connect. I take a moment to ground and become centered. And I ask. What is this pain? What do I need to know? I hear it. I question it for a moment, but I know I need to trust it. I know when I trust it, Miracles happen. Transformation and shifts happen. Two and a half years into doing this not just daily, but as a lifestyle and I still had a moment of doubt. The difference is I know which voice to listen to. I allow myself to trust and to override that doubt.

Phew, that was some deep stuff I wasn't expecting to come up today. I'm taking a moment to show gratitude for this new awareness. I pray and ask for Miracles for it to be released and to be shown the way to move forward. I'm already feeling better. I will further support myself today with a self-reiki/hands-on healing session in an Epsom salt bath. Infused with essential oils, crystal healing, and high vibe music. I am trusting. I am allowing. I am being authentic. I am thriving.

As you continue to further define your authentic core beliefs, align your mindset and align your actions, you will see your personalized lifestyle of balanced wellness come to life. Your ability to manifest will not change. You are a powerful creator. However, your ability to manifest in alignment with your destiny and life purpose will be undeniable. And when things are not showing up as you are wanting, it's important to check in and do the work.

Serenity Maven Activity #15 - Identifying Blocks and Fears

This is an activity to check and take an inventory of your blocks and any fears. What are the blocks holding you back from trusting right now?

Connect, center, balance, and ground. Write all the things that come up - even if it seems silly, write it down.

Example: Mama Honey's authentic fears in this very moment

Blocks/Fears	Positive Affirmation
I am not perfect	I am enough. I am supported by God and the universe.
What if people judge the areas I've not yet worked on?	I am on my own path. I was chosen to shine my light.
What if I make the wrong choice?	I am always supported.
What if it all works out, and I have nothing to complain about?	I am full of peace, flow, and happiness I desire.
What if it works out, and then I fail? I don't get to keep what I have created?	I am divinely guided on my path and journey. I surrender and allow myself to receive.
What if others don't agree or like what I know is right for me?	I cut the cords with those who have attached their egos expectations of my life purpose and mission. I know what is best for myself. I allow others to make their own life choices in support of their life purpose and mission
What if my kids are disappointed?	I am supported by my tribe. I am valued by others, just as I value myself. I am invaluable. I am healing, so my family is healing.

What if my message is not accepted?	I am meant to be heard by those who are chosen to be in my path. I am open to trusting that those who need it will receive it. I believe in my life purpose and mission.
What if I don't have the answers?	I teach what I live. I am truth.

My new affirmation:

I am enough. I am supported by my God of Understanding/Universe/Spirit/Source.

I am on my own path. I was chosen to shine my light.

I am always supported.

I am full of peace, flow, and happiness I desire.

I am divinely guided on my path and journey. I surrender and allow myself to receive.

I cut the cords with those who have attached their egos expectations of my life purpose and mission. I know what is best for myself. I allow others to make their own life choices in support of their life purpose and mission.

I am supported by my tribe. I am valued by others, just as I value myself. I am invaluable. I am healing, so my family is healing.

I am meant to be heard by those who are chosen to be in my path. I am open to trusting that those who need it will receive it. I believe in my life purpose and mission.

I teach what I live. I am truth.

I am enough. I am supported by God and the universe.
I am on my own path. I was chosen to shine my light.
I am always supported.
I am full of peace, flow, and happiness I desire.
I am divinely guided on my path and journey.
I surrender and allow myself to receive.
I cut the cords with those who have attached their egos expectations of my life purpose and mission.
I know what is best for myself.
I allow others to make their own life choices in support of their life purpose and mission.
I am supported by my tribe.
I am valued by others, just as I value myself.
I am invaluable.
I am healing so my family is healing.
I am meant to be heard by those who are chosen to be in my path.
I am open to trusting that those who need it will receive it.
I believe in my life purpose and mission.
I teach what I live. I am truth.

Your blocks and fears	Your positive affirmation (opposite of your fears)

Serenity Maven Tip: *What if the pain and sickness you have is the result of anger and rage not that the anger* *and rage is a result of the pain and sickness? Now that you have the tools to connect and release. Can your quality of life improve? What will you put in place to remember why this important to you? More than food for thought. Check-in and take aligned action.*

PS - Sometimes, miracles show up by way of those who are practitioners of western medicine and/or alternative practitioners.

Chapter 10

CONTINUE LIVING A BALANCED WELLNESS LIFESTYLE

Dear one, you did it! You got to the last chapter of **The Serenity Maven's Guide to Balanced Wellness**. I am sooooo happy for you, for our Serenity Maven community, for our planet! You are now officially in the midst of a new level on your healing journey.

Your journey will forever be enriched from this experience, by your choice to commit to being self-centered. Each time you show up for yourself and raise your own vibe, you raise the vibe of the planet. YOU are purposeful. YOUR JOURNEY is healing your own family, past and future generations, and lives around the world. As those around you see you heal, they are not only inspired by they are also healing.

Let's take a moment for a refresh of what the healing, phases, cycle, and steps are to living a lifestyle of balanced wellness to achieve your targeted wellbeing.

Phases of the healing journey:
Phase 1 - Cleansing
Phase 2 - Re-energizing
Phase 3 - Changing Present Life Patterns & Family Patterns
Phase 4 - Changing Past Life Patterns
Phase 5 - Manifestation in alignment with your Best Self

Cycle of Targeted Wellbeing:
Balanced Wellness of Spirit, Mind, & Body
Defining Your Core Beliefs
Aligning Your Mindset
Aligning Your Actions

Steps to Balanced Wellness

1. Decide
2. Create A Peaceful Space
3. Connect
4. Intention
5. Centered, Focused, & Grounded
6. Living in the moment
7. Release the past
8. Envision the future
9. Trust Yourself
10. Continue

As a Serenity Maven yourself, you have completed these Serenity Maven Activities to and you now have new awareness and perspectives.

#1 - Inventory Time
#2: Working Through Resistance
#3 - Connecting to Your Core Authentic Beliefs
#4 - Getting Real with Yourself

#5 - Creating Sacred Space at Work
#6 - Creating Sacred Space at Home
#7 - Setting Sacred Space Everywhere
#8 - Creating Sacred Space Now
#9 - Cutting Cords
#10 - Your Awareness Level
#11 - Intentional Living
#12 - Connected Free Writing
#13 - Ground and Center
#14 - Envision Your Future and Best Self
#15 - Identifying Blocks and Fears
#16 - The Difference Between Your Intuition and & Your Fears
#17 - Being Happy, Balanced & Authentic

With your deep understanding of the steps, the healing cycles and phases will all fall into place. Your job and responsibility are to now continue to live an authentic life. Here are the daily actions required to continue to live a lifestyle of balanced wellness.

- DAILY SELFCARE
- AFFIRMATIONS -Use daily affirmations that you personally create based on your vision for your life and who you need to be to create that life. Reprogram your own mind in alignment with your core beliefs.
- LIVE IN THE MOMENT - Take action that is intuitively guided, without judgment or fears.
- HEAL YOUR INNER CHILD - Actively work on responding vs. reacting. Delve more into the world of chakras and more!
- CONNECT WITH COMMUNITY - Create a community with friendships and support of like-minded people. Get involved in your community.
- CREATE BALANCED WELLNESS and ACHIEVE TARGETED WELLBEING-Through living a lifestyle of

balanced wellness you have personalized for your own happiness
- AMPLIFY - You're also invited to up level your own support by learning new or additional alternative and complementary practices such as Healing Touch, Reiki, Crystal Healing, Guided Imagery, Hypnotherapy, EFT, EERT, and more! Follow your heart and own intuition.

Here is a divinely timed intuitive message just for you, for right now, and every time you read it.

You are the light of the world. You are so needed, and everything that you have been through up until now has prepared you for this very moment, an opportunity to shine even brighter. All throughout the day each and every single day, you have a choice, a choice to take authentic action. Each choice is an opportunity to fall back on habits and behaviors that you've created as a way of surviving of coping, and just getting by or to choose to live purposefully.

To life knowing that no matter what happens or what others think, that you made a choice to do what was right for you. What regrets do you have? The time you followed your initial gut instinct or the times you overrode that. When you look back over your lifetime up to this point, those moments that lead to shame and guilt and sadness and anger depression are directly those tied to those moments that you didn't Follow Your Truth, or perhaps you were prevented from your truth. I have no other explanation I can accept in these situations, other than we signed up for this lifetime and knew of the lessons. I've also heard that some situations in this lifetime were chosen, others are as a result of choices. You're invited to check-in when this comes up and ask your best self the answers for you.

As with all my clients and students, you are aware and allowing yourself to learn the lessons that are necessary for you to make big changes and big commitments. Your specific life purpose requires your special and unique experiences. Including your hardships and trials. There are so many people that can relate to you. By simply showing up as your authentic self, by simply changing your own vibration to evolve, those who are connected to you will either be drawn to rise with you. Some will be resistance and put their head further in the sand. But dear one, you recognize what this looks like because you too have been in this space of being unaware and asleep. As you awaken, at times, it may feel hard to move forward. You may also feel torn by how you feel. Healing is not all roses, and great feelings all the time. Healing is about raising your vibration to love, so you can navigate the shitty truths.

Just the other day, I called this mixed feeling the undertow. There is a flow happening on the surface, but under the surface, the terrain is changing. This change is felt and has to be acknowledged. When the whispers/pressures of this awareness come in, be gentle. Rest. Take care of yourself. Be open to understanding how the change will benefit you.

Be aware of resistance. Resistance is when you know something is for you, but blocks are coming up, such as fears. You may catch yourself going on autopilot as a way to avoid what you know and want or distract you from the aligned path.

RESISTANCE VS. KNOWING AND INTUITION

Resistance is different than when something is not for you. When something is not for you, your intuition is strong, loving no, with your ego/thoughts trying to convince you otherwise. When something (a situation, person/relationship, place/home/travel, job/career/life purpose, anything) is for you, you will know.

You can physically feel the difference in your body and where the feelings come from. You can check in now and try it.

Serenity Maven Activity #16 - The Difference Between Your Intuition and & Your Fears

Place one had on your lower belly and one hand on your upper belly. Your lower belly is your intuition. Your upper belly is where your fears are. Check-in with the feeling once you connect with them. Feel them. Ask what they are. Allow it to come up and out. Then pray and ask for a Miracle healing and to know what is the next step for you. Then take that action.

AWESOME!!!!! Wow!! How amazing was that? You are trusting yourself so much now! Most important is to align your actions. You may not be "perfect" according to your old standards, but you are surely being authentic as you allow the divine timing of your own healing to unfold.

Dear one. You are ready to step up. To show up even bigger and bolder. You have the tools to continue to up-level as you continue to shine your bright light on this world. Those who may feel like you're leaving them behind on your journey are just behind you. They are watching you and are needing you to show up. They are inspired by you just as you are with those who have stepped up to the call before you.

Think of all the times before this where you've had the opportunity to say yes. You instead allowed the voice of negativity to hold you back. Or perhaps had opportunities to say no, and you allowed obligations to get in the way. This very moment, right now, is a gem opportunity of awareness and time for you to be curious. For you to be gentle and for you to be the f****** real deal FOR YOURSELF! Did you hear me? Like it's time to get real. Deep real truths, the shitty ones and all. No one else is going to do it for you. No one else is going to show up for you the way that you must show up for yourself. And as a dutiful reminder, dear one, you are now responsible for stepping into action based on your awareness.

It's time. Your future is now. You are creating your future in this moment very moment and every moment.

Serenity Maven Activity #17 - Being Happy, Balanced & Authentic

Your final Serenity Maven Activity is to go out into the world. To BE YOU! To BE LOVE! And to SHINE BRIGHT like only you were meant to uniquely shine!

Sending you lots of healing light and love,

Xoxo
Mama Honey

> *Your Final Serenity Maven Tip* - The activities in this guidebook are timeless. They can be repeated when you are drawn to it. Set the intention now to be called back when needed. Your future self will thank you!

About the Author

International Speaker & Author Honey-Marie, known as Mama Honey, the Serenity Maven, is an inner child healing expert who helps professionals shift from surviving to thriving. She is an intuitive transformational life coach who teaches alternative healing modalities at the Targeted Wellbeing Center's School of Intuitive Healing. Honey is the mother of five who uses these steps as a way of living an intuitive lifestyle.

Before learning these steps and how to trust and follow her own heart's desires and intuition, Honey lived a life full of fear. Most times finding herself paralyzed, from what others would think of her. When she did move forward, it was at the expense of her personal happiness. It was after her youngest daughter was born with a rare genetic mutation, that her life came spiraling to a halt from obsessing over what her daughter needed and throwing herself into being busy and neglecting her own needs.

Now claiming a lifestyle of thriving, after claiming the life of a survivor for decades, she has removed her survivor badge that limited herself thoughts and actions. Mama Honey is a former survivor of being orphaned as a teenager, a two-time teen mom, relationships with narcissistic abuse (intimate and non-intimate), and a marriage full of toxic verbal, emotional, and physical abuse that almost cost her life. Today Mama Honey embodies thriving as a state of being, and when she is out of alignment, the tools in this guidebook continue to be her go-to way of working through what comes up.

STAY CONNECTED

Website: TargetedWellbeingCenter.com
Facebook Community: Serenity Mavens & Serenity Maven Mamas
Facebook Page: Mama Honey, the Serenity Maven
Instagram: mamahoneyserenitymaven
Podcast: iTunes & Spotify: Finding Mommy's Soft Voice - Family Healing with Mama Honey

To access your Serenity Maven Tool Box go to:
http://bit.ly/serenitymaventoolbox

Your Serenity Maven Tool Box includes:

- Serenity Maven Gift: The Serenity Maven's 8 Day Chakra Challenge
- The Serenity Maven's Meditation Library, including:
  - Serenity Maven Activity #9 - Guided Meditation: Cord Cutting Meditation
  - Serenity Maven Activity #14 - Guided Imagery Session: Envisioning Your Future
- Links to Photographs from the Frozen Water, Rice, and Salt, Water, Vinegar experiments
- Access to LIVE and recorded events - including New Moon and Full Moon Meditations
- Access to book a private session (online sessions - available around the globe)

Made in the USA
Lexington, KY
15 December 2019